W9-CDC-750

Limited Edition Hardbound $30.00
with Price Guide

Encyclopedia of
Victorian Colored Pattern Glass
Book 9

Cranberry Opalescent from A to Z

by

william heacock & william gamble

Editor
Tom Klopp

Photography by
Rebecca VanBrackel & Deana Tullius

Copyright 1987
by
Antique Publications
P.O. Box 553
Marietta, Ohio 45750

Dedication
To David Richardson

For 10 years of friendship and
support, and without whom my
work could not continue

Paperbound I.S.B.N. #0-915410-23-0
Hardbound I.S.B.N. #0-915410-24-9

INTRODUCTION BY WILLIAM HEACOCK

Whereas the glass shown in this book in color is almost exclusively cranberry opalescent, this is a book on ALL the blown opalescent patterns, many of which are incorrectly identified by my primitive research in Book 2 of this series—OPALESCENT GLASS FROM A TO Z. Since that book was published first in 1975, so much more has been learned from the accessibility of trade journals, primarily from The Corning Museum of Glass and the Library of Congress. This information was too important to await any proposed revision of Book 2, and since a number of patterns had been discovered since 1975, I believed a separate publication on the blown patterns was warranted. With the cooperation of long-time friend and research contributor William Gamble, and the profound generosity of a number of other collectors who believed in this new volume, I decided to present these new findings in this book prior to my planned books on Northwood.

I mention this Northwood TRILOGY in this introduction because Harry Northwood's contributions to the production of opalescent, and in particular blown opalescent, are superior to those of any other individual in America's glass history. My co-author on this trilogy, involving three separate works on Northwood's early (1882-1902) and later (1902-1925) production is Berry Wiggins, author of STRETCH IN COLOR. The third volume in that series will be on the Indiana, Pa. factory that Northwood left in 1899, but which continued to produce glass which has been confused for "Northwood" for many years.

Much blown opalescent glass was made at the various Northwood factories and at the factories where Mr. Northwood worked (Phoenix, Hobbs, La Belle, Buckeye), so this book can be considered something of a large "chapter" preparing readers for the deeply personal and complicated history of these different firms. But the Northwood trilogy will be much more than a historical record of companies and glass. It will be my first attempt to create a biographical work of some note, on a man and his family, and the powerful contributions he made in the creative art of glassmaking. It will involve hundreds of personal records, photographs, letters, deeds, wills, and interviews with surviving family members. Mr. Wiggins and I have been gathering data for more than ten years for these important works, and now, with the aid of computers and the full cooperation of the Northwood family, this testament to a great glass genius can become a reality.

Blown opalescent glassmaking techniques, in essence, came to America from England, arriving on the boat when Harry Northwood, at age 21, stepped onto our shores. He immediately went to Wheeling, possibly to join his cousin Thomas Dugan who was also working there in 1881, and as a trade journal noted, he showed the workers there glassmaking techniques never before utilized commercially in America.

The oft told tale of cranberry color being accidentally discovered when a worker dropped a gold coin into a boiling batch of crystal could not be further from the truth. This color is an overlay, requiring a layer of crystal coated with a layer of cranberry, and then blown into shape. It requires strict temperature control and cannot be made successfully in pressed form. It must be a blown pattern to have the true pink coloration for which it is known.

Cranberry opalescent was originally called "ruby opalescent" or "pink opalescent" in the early trade journals and catalogues. The use of the term "cranberry glass", much like the glass terms "custard" and "carnival", was introduced by the antiques collectors—not the glass industry. The first commercial production of the color in America appears to have gained momentum in 1884. The English-bred glassworkers at the Mt. Washington Glass Works and the Phoenix Glass Co. were competing at this time for the art glass market. The Hobbs, Brockunier concern at Wheeling joined in immediately. The trade journals for the mid-1880's are clearly filled with references to colors like "Peach Blow", "Coral" and "Amberina", but these colors were not excluded to single factories. Neither was the color "ruby" (cranberry). The workers apparently moved from factory to factory, carrying with them valuable formulas and glassmaking secrets, which made it possible for other manufacturers to compete with popular, marketable production colors. We collectors tend to think of the final product as a work of glassmaking craftsmanship, which it is, but we lose sight of the fact that it was also originally a commercially manufactured product conceived by businessmen to make a profit. A number of patents and lawsuits are recorded during this period, as manufacturers sought to protect their ideas, usually with little success. Other companies which made "ruby" color during the 1880's include New England Glass Works, La Belle, Geo. Duncan & Sons, and Northwood's own factory which opened in 1888.

Thus we note the problem in attributing many of the patterns shown in this book. With very few ads and catalogues available which illustrate this glass, naming manufacturers can sometimes be a matter of comparing colors and molds to existing attributable items. In a few cases, naming the maker is virtually impossible. It becomes a matter of eliminating the obvious and focusing on the most likely possibilities, particularly on the staple designs known as COINSPOT, SWIRL and STRIPE. Just about every factory making blown opalescent was using these patterns. These three are particularly difficult to research.

The items pictured in black and white are in ALL colors of blown opalescent, not only cranberry. If the color is known, it is noted. But some of these items were pictured originally (over the past ten years) in black and white, and the original color may not have been noted by me at the time. Such cases are rare, but are important, as some manufacturers may not have made cranberry opalescent. It appears that the Model Flint Glass Co. at Albany, Ind., made their lines only in blue, yellow and flint (white) opalescent.

INTRODUCTION BY WILLIAM GAMBLE

Cranberry! The ultimate color of opalescent pattern glass. Cranberry opalescent was made in a wide variety of shapes. Cruet, syrup and toothpick collectors highly regard their cranberry examples as some of the finest pieces made. Even art glass collectors highly prize the so-called Raspberry Onyx production—which was cranberry opalescent glassware with a satin finish.

All old cranberry opalescent glassware was blown. These patterns are not pressed. Therefore they seldom reveal mold lines. These frequently melt out from the refiring process. Because most of these pieces were blown in a mold for the pattern of opalescence, then in another mold for shape, the opalescent design in the glass will not always fall in the same position on a given piece.

The lemonade or water set seems to be the most prolific item in cranberry opalescent. The table set pieces (butter, sugar, creamer and spooner) are much more difficult to find. Amongst the table set items, the spooner appears more frequently today. This spooner was a vessel which was well suited to fit into a silvered frame, forming a pickle caster. Often the crimped bowls were also fitted into silvered frames, making beautiful brides' baskets. The toothpick, alone or in combination with the cruet, salt and pepper, can also be found in silver-plated frames. Often the colors of cranberry, white, blue and yellow opalescent were housed in the same holder.

The seasoning set pieces (cruet, syrup, toothpick, sugar shaker and salt shaker) are difficult to find. They sometimes demand premium prices on the rarer patterns.

I hope this book will serve as a guide for you in your search for some of the finest examples of Victorian colored pattern glass—cranberry opalescent.

ACKNOWLEDGEMENTS

First and foremost, I must thank my co-author, William Gamble, who first presented the idea for this book to me and pursued its publication. He gathered the glass from his own personal collection, and solicited other collectors across the Midwest to send their glass to him for the arduous photography at Marietta. He presented a manuscript with his own observations as a collector and dealer, which included valuable "field research" concerning shapes, finials, colors, shape molds, bases and reproductions. This is presented in the book under "COLLECTOR'S NOTES". Sometimes we did not agree on our points, so an occasional "point/counterpoint" will appear in the text. My own observations are presented under "RESEARCH NOTES" or simply "NOTES". Combining Mr. Gamble's facts with my own research from trade journals, an important contribution to glass history could be prepared.

After the initial photography, we realized there was room for much more, and decided to expand the book to include cranberry opalescent from the recent years. Joe and Audrey Humphrey unselfishly offered to pack and remove hundreds of pieces from their home, travelling to the Marietta, Ohio, photography studio. Here they unpacked the glass, helped arrange it for each color shot, noted important measurements, and provided me with information they had learned in their collecting endeavors. Audrey is known around Ohio as "The Cranberry Kid", and her love for the glass extends from the very old to the very recent Fenton production. She attends hundreds of auctions and was very important in advising on the prices realized on Fenton and L.G. Wright cranberry opalescent.

Many other collectors and dealers were involved in this book through the loaning of glass, some of whom packed a dozen or more examples to mail to us for photography in color. Taking such risks deserves special mention. The postal system had to be trusted not once, but twice, as the glass was mailed back to them (by my co-author, Mr. Gamble). The list below seems a feeble method of sincerely thanking these generous individuals and couples. Mr. Gamble and I both truly appreciate their involvement in a book in which we hope they will be proud of their participation.

Robert & Jean Brocke
Jim Broom
Jack Burke
Virginia Ellison
Dorothy Frazee
Steve Gehring
Ray & Jennie Goldsberry
John & Eve Gordon
Leonard & Marie Gyles

Chuck Hardy
Norman & Noreen Koch
Lawrence Loxterman
Joan McGee
Tom Neale
Mr. & Mrs. Les Norman
Ward Rohm
Glen & Juanita Wilkins

Our sincere thanks to Steve Jennings for reprint permission from an L.G. Wright Glass Co. catalogue and to Frank M. Fenton for reprints of Fenton Art Glass Co. catalogues. The cranberry glass sold since 1939 by both of these firms (all of it made by Fenton) has kept the Victorian traditions alive for new generations of glass lovers. This glass is highly collectible today and increasing rapidly in value. For early trade journal ads, we thank the helpful staff of the Rakow Library at the Corning Museum of Glass, Corning, N.Y.

MAIN PATTERN MOTIFS

The pattern motifs are separated by type into a variety of categories, making comparison of copies and look-alikes simpler for readers. The general categories are:

COINSPOTS (Ribbed, Plain, Coinspot & Swirl, Bull's Eye)
FLOWERS & FERNS (Daisy & Fern, Poinsettia, Fern, Scottish Moor)
GEOMETRICS (Honeycomb, Diamonds, Herringbone, Swastika)
POLKA DOTS (Windows, Polka Dot, Big Windows)
ROCOCOS (Alhambra, Spanish Lace, Seaweed, Buttons/Braids, Arabian Nights)
LATTICES (Criss-Cross, Buckeye Lattice, Ribbed Opal Lattice)
STRIPES (Stripe, Wide Stripe)
SWIRLS (Rings, Reverse Swirl, Chrysanthemum Swirl, Plain Swirl)
MISCELLANEOUS (Hobnail, Stars & Stripes, Drapery, Twist, Christmas Snowflake)

Because of the overlap in attributions, it is important that I point out in this introduction that it was impossible for each and every piece pictured in the generic lines COINSPOT, STRIPE, SWIRL and LATTICE to be pinpointed for attribution. If we could do that, we could have patterns called "Nickel's Stripe", "Hobbs' Stripe", "Northwood's Stripe" and "Beaumont's Stripe". Unfortunately, molds were sometimes relocated, factories changed owners and names, designs and shapes were copied, workers and designers moved from location to location. If an item is called "Northwood", collectors must note that he had four different factories and worked at four others. Also, his molds were used by other firms. Percy Beaumont designed for Hobbs, West Virginia and his own two factories. An item called "Beaumont" could have been made earlier in the same or a different shape by Hobbs or West Virginia Glass. Some items are merely listed under the known shapes with no discussion in the text whatsoever. Either no maker was known, or it was an unfortunate oversight. The price guide is planned to include a quick attribution update reference every two or so years as it is revised.

SHAPE MOLDS

Other than providing attributions on blown opalescent glass, perhaps even more difficult is providing standard nomenclatures for the patterns and the shape molds in which they are found. After all, a single opalescent design can be found in five or six different shape variations, and each one can be from a different company. At first, I toyed with the idea of a numerical system for all the different shape molds in which the water pitchers are found. Then I realized that such a numerical system was being provided by the figure numbers used in the color section. If you find an item not shown in this book, search for the shape mold. Any reference to that item then can be explained by the pattern motif matching a particular shape in this book.

Some shape molds have pattern names of their own, and most are listed below. These molds can be found in colors and with decorations other than an opalescent motif. All of these molds are blown-glass molds, not press molds.

RIBBED PILLAR mold — Northwood at Ellwood City and Indiana, Pa.

PANELLED SPRIG — Northwood at Ellwood City and Indiana, Pa.

NORTHWOOD SWIRL — Used on Royal Ivy, Parian Swirl, Daisy & Fern, Coinspot & Swirl, by Northwood at Martin's Ferry and Ellwood City

JEWEL ("Threaded Rubina Swirl") — Opalescent SWIRL salt shaker at Martin's Ferry (primarily made in plain Rubina color)

APPLE BLOSSOM — Northwood at Indiana, Pa. (main line in decorated milk glass)

RIBBON TIE mold — Spanish Lace tankard and salt shakers, Northwood at Indiana, Pa., possibly continued by National Glass

UTOPIA OPTIC — shape molds used on SPANISH LACE (Northwood at Indiana, Pa.)

BULBOUS BASE — A Hobbs shape mold used on a Frances Ware decorated line and also with an inside Optic pattern. Mold may have also been used by Northwood after 1902

MULTI-RIBBED ROSE BOWL — yellow opalescent SEAWEED example known

BALL-SHAPED syrup — Spanish Lace, Daisy & Fern (beware of repros), Swastika, Coinspot, Coinspot & Swirl

FANCY FANS — a line in opal ware from Northwood's Ellwood City factory, used on POLKA DOT pattern

OVAL INDIANA cruet mold — Spanish Lace, Daisy & Fern, COINSPOT (beware of repros)

RING NECK (water pitcher, sugar shaker, syrup, cruet, toothpick) Used on STRIPE, COINSPOT, and in Rubina and cased Vasa Murrhina (PRIMA DONNA)

NINE PANEL SYRUP & SUGAR SHAKER — Swirl, Stripe, Coinspot, Daisy & Fern, Blown Twist, Spanish Lace

WIDE-WAIST SUGAR SHAKER — Swirl, Stripe, Coinspot, Daisy & Fern, Blown Twist, Spanish Lace (same patterns as NINE PANEL)

HOBBS' SWIRL — No. 326 mold (used on Frances Ware Swirl line)

WEST VIRGINIA OPTIC — Used on DAISY & FERN, POLKA DOT FERN by West Virginia Glass Co. in 1893-1894

BUCKEYE SWIRL — Used on table pieces in REVERSE SWIRL and BIG WINDOWS, both by Buckeye Glass Co., but also possibly made at American Glass Co.; these molds also used for non-opalescent speckled glass and opaque glass

BLOWN OPALESCENT AFTER 1905
ARE THEY REPRODUCTIONS?

The peak production years of blown opalescent tableware and novelties were from about 1884 to 1904, about a twenty year period. However, a limited amount appeared from time to time on the market. No cranberry opalescent was made by Fenton Art Glass Co. until the 1930's. From 1910-20 this firm made three opalescent water sets in flint, green and blue opalescent with pressed tumblers in the COIN-SPOT, SWIRL and BUTTONS AND BRAIDS patterns. These were copies of sets made earlier by Frank Fenton's former employer, Jefferson Glass Co., a firm which did make cranberry before 1910.

In the 1920's, a few lemonade sets were made in blown opalescent, but none in cranberry. These were usually with the popular ice-lip of the period, or with lids. The tumblers were always iced-tea size, taller than those of the Victorian period.

In 1939, the Fenton Art Glass Co. brought out a major line of opalescent SWIRL, DOT, STRIPE and WIDE STRIPE in vases, bowls and other shapes, in colors of blue, yellow, flint and cranberry opalescent. These were abandoned after a single year in the line, so most are extremely rare today and command prices—especially in cranberry—comparable to prices of much earlier glass. These lines all had their own original Fenton names which differed from the Victorian glass names. Their SPIRAL OPTIC is our SWIRL, their WIDE RIB is our WIDE STRIPE. These are clearly listed in our Fenton reprints.

At about this time, L.G. Wright, a road salesman for the New Martinsville Glass Co., learned of a warehouse of old molds from the glass factory at Indiana, Pa., and amongst them were molds from the Northwood, Dugan and Diamond Glass companies which had operated there. He purchased these molds and took one, the HOBNAIL barber bottle (Fig. 304), to Fenton at Williamstown, and had a number of these bottles made in the cranberry opalescent which Fenton was producing at the time. Frank Fenton got the idea for his own HOBNAIL line of ware from this bottle, and the rest is history. The Fenton company has produced HOBNAIL in one form or another ever since, and its name has become associated with the design.

Thus, an original Northwood mold (itself a reproduction of a Hobbs, Brockunier mold) continued to influence the production of glass well into the 20th century. When Fenton produced their successful HOBNAIL, other firms were producing competing lines. Fenton's molds were entirely new shapes distinctive to the company, and this was the only firm to produce a line in cranberry opalescent since 1940. The HOBNAIL which Duncan & Miller called "cranberry pink" was more of a salmon color, and Frank M. Fenton recalls his uncle's amusement at the competition calling this color "cranberry". Duncan's ads after 1940 call this color "peach", which is more descriptive.

There was other cranberry HOBNAIL on the market just prior to this time from Czechoslovakia. Other opalescent designs, particularly SWIRL and STRIPE, have also been spotted with acid stamped marks "Made in Czechoslovakia". When World War 2 broke out in Europe, a hungry market for this color and design must have opened up. The Czech HOBNAIL, and the Fenton and D&M HOBNAIL, are relatively easy to find on today's collectors' market, indicating extensive and lengthy production.

Since the late 1930's, The Fenton Art Glass Co. has been doing contract work for L.G. Wright Glass Co., at New Martinsville, and has produced all of this firm's cranberry opalescent and cased colors. First relying heavily on the old Indiana, Pa. molds, the Wright concern had additional hundreds of molds made to expand its line of gift and novelty glass over the years. Many of the items found in cranberry opalescent are in shapes never originally made, and are easy to distinguish from the old. But when an original Northwood/Dugan/Diamond mold is used, it becomes more difficult for beginning collectors to avoid paying an "antique" price for a reproduction. The distinctive "melon rib" shape found on many Wright cranberry pieces was apparently taken from an old Beaumont Glass Co. bitters bottle and expanded to include other shapes (pitchers, lamps, open sugars, etc.). The L.G. Wright pressed glass was made at a variety of factories, including Fenton, Westmoreland, Viking and Imperial.

Fortunately, depending upon your perspective, the high collectability of cranberry opalescent, and Fenton glass in general, has led to a revived interest in collecting the copies made since 1938. The new, limited edition, cranberry opalescent being made by Fenton today is very expensive to produce, and an awareness of this fact has led many collectors to seek out, whereas they formerly avoided, the L.G. Wright items.

The Steuben Glass Works at Corning, N. Y., produced a line of cranberry opalescent in the 1930's under the auspices of Frederick Carder, another Englishman from the Stourbridge area. Much glass was made here in the style of the early English Victorian period. The opalescent glass is very lightweight, usually has a polished pontil, and is styled in the contemporary shapes of the period. *Revi AANG, p. 166* lists colors of cranberry, green and orchid opalescent. The cranberry was called "Oriental Poppy". When finished with a lustre surface inside and out it is called CLOUDED GLASS. The "Swirl" and "Stripe" motifs were primarily used. Revi indicates it is never signed.

Book 9 concentrates primarily on American production, but a few examples from England and the Continent are included for comparison only. Cranberry opalescent was made in England from about 1880 to as late as the 1930's.

I have gone on record in the past with some fairly harsh statements about reproductions and the harm they do to collectors' investments. But since I entered the 20th Century with my research, and have expanded my "boundaries" in glass history, and have seen one famous factory after another close its doors forever, I have begun to appreciate all glass for what it is. If it is a reproduction, then it should be represented and sold as one. The reproduction was made with the same care, and considerably more expense, than the original was made one hundred years ago. It is this high cost of fuel and labor, as well as the competition from cheaply made, government subsidized, foreign glass, that is hurting our struggling American glass industry. When something becomes scarce, it becomes more precious to the beholder. Some day all glass may come from foreign shores, and you will then perhaps understand how special hand-made American glass is—no matter how old it is.

HOW WAS BLOWN OPALESCENT GLASS MADE?

Cranberry opalescent is a color which cannot be pressed successfully. The color requires exacting temperature control not compatible with pressing techniques. I am not a glass technician, but in my own words I will try to explain how it is made.

First, a "gather" of molten cranberry glass is attached to the end of a blow pipe. This glass is then coated with an outer layer of clear glass which has bone ash in the formula. This unformed ball of glass is then blown into the "spot" mold. This spot mold has the basic design of the pattern in relief, that portion of the final piece which is white (opalescent). The formed object is then removed from the mold, still attached to the blow pipe, and then reheated in the glory hole of the furnace (this reheating turns the raised portions of the glass white). At this point the hot glass is immediately reblown into a "shape" mold. The mold is opened, the formed object removed, and the piece is again reheated in the glory hole at the top in order to crimp or "finish" the rim. If you carefully examine a piece of cranberry opalescent, especially an item with a polished top (like a tumbler), you will see the two layers of glass, the cranberry interior and the crystal opalescent exterior.

The few attempts at pressing cranberry have been by Fenton in recent years (1950's and later). These examples tend to end up with a deep purple cast. Three items shown in this book (Figures 233, 329 and 376) have this odd color. These items could have been blown, but I believe they were pressed. None have polished pontil. However, it should be remembered that not all blown glass carries a pontil scar at the bottom (where the pontil was attached). Many items were held with other special devices while the rough rim was reheated and "finished" with a crimp or smoothed edge. There may be some disagreement between the authors of this book concerning the importance of a polished pontil scar on the base of the glass piece. On this fact, however, we

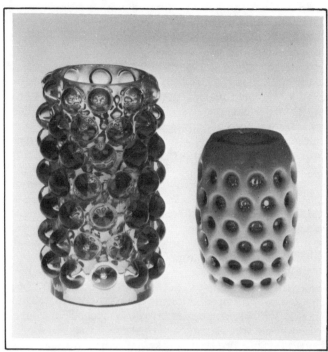

These oddly shaped pieces were blown from spot molds but never blown into a shape mold. On the left is a piece from a DOT OPTIC (COINSPOT) mold, never opalized, and on the right is an unformed piece from a COIN DOT spot mold, refired for opalescence. Courtesy Frank M. Fenton

do agree—the earliest cranberry opalescent by Hobbs, Phoenix and La Belle (circa 1885-1890) usually has a pontil scar.

The photograph here, courtesy of Frank Fenton, shows a piece formed from a Fenton COIN DOT spot mold (reheated but not reblown) next to a piece of glass blown in a DOT OPTIC spot mold.

THE REEDED AND TWISTED HANDLES

Most cranberry opalescent has a plain, clear glass, applied handle. Reeded handles found on most reproductions have caused some collectors to avoid any pieces found with this handle. The term "avoid or beware of reeded handles" was designed for beginning collectors who are looking for simple answers. But investing in glass is not that simple. It requires a considerable amount of study, and even the "experts" like us are learning new rules every day.

The early art glass made in America, produced by such fine manufacturers as Hobbs, Brockunier & Co., Mt. Washington, New England, Phoenix, Duncan and others, was made in the style used by many young glassworkers induced

to this country from England. For many years, some of these pieces were considered to be English. But we now have more knowledge at our disposal, and we know many pitchers and oil cruets with reeded handles are indeed American-made from the 1880's. Almost all pieces from this period have polished pontils at the base. Examples of early glass with reeded handles can be seen in this book, Figures 231, 228, 230 and 248.

The "twisted" handle is a variation of the reeded handle. See Figs. 95, 175 and 183, all water pitchers known made by Northwood.

NOTES ON THE SEASONING SERVICE

The Victorian oil cruet was an important part of the seasoning set. Because of its importance, the cruet was used extensively—thus it suffered a multitude of abuse. The pouring spouts were frequently chipped, the handle could become cracked, and the stopper could easily be dropped and broken.

Original stoppers cannot be easily determined—especially in the blown glass cruets. Pressed pattern cruets often have a matching pattern stopper or a pressed stopper of uniform dimension. The blown cruet most frequently includes a cut glass stopper. It is difficult to say if the cut stopper in any given blown cranberry opalescent cruet is original. If the stopper fits the neck of the cruet well, if the top of the stopper is not too large or too small, if the shank (or neck) of the stopper is not too close or too far away from the top of the cruet—all of these factors determine whether the stopper can be considered original. It takes experience in seeing and handling Victorian cruets over a long period of time. One might say it takes an "eye" to judge the originality of a cruet's stopper.

Original catalogues have helped us determine the originality of cruet stoppers, but even these could have been changed over the production life of a particular pattern. We know the Hobbs, Brockunier & Co. used special cut stoppers (often in color) in their blown pattern cruets. It appears Northwood used pressed glass stoppers in some of his blown cruets.

Most blown cranberry opalescent cruets, with few exceptions, have plain applied clear handles. The SPANISH LACE cruet is one notable exception. This cruet always seems to have a reeded handle. Examples with colored handles in amber or blue are probably English or Bohemian.

Victorian blown cruets will have basically two styles of pouring spouts: either a pulled out lip or a tri-corner spout. I know of no Victorian cruet with a ruffled spout. The STARS AND STRIPES (Fig. 165) and the BLOWN DRAPERY (Fig. 184) are probably not cruets made during the Victorian period. They are highly collectible items, apparently made in limited quantity, that were made at a date later than the patterns' original production period (1890-1902). I am not certain of their origin at this time, but feel they were a product of the L.G. Wright Glass Co. in the early 1940's or 1950's, prior to this firm's introduction of catalogues. All L.G. Wright cranberry opalescent was made by the Fenton Art Glass Co.

There is nothing wrong with having "collectible" glass in a cranberry opalescent collection. But don't be duped into paying Victorian prices for a recently produced item. These collectible cruets and other shapes sold for as much as $25.00 retail in the 1950's. You should be the judge as to how much more you wish to pay for them in the 1980's. Age has little to do with the value of glass. But in most cases, collectibility is the determining factor in an item's value. It is usually the dealer who does not take the time to study or invest in reference books who is asking a Victorian glass price for glass of recent issue.

The Victorian syrup remains one of the most highly collectible items in the seasoning set. The metal tops, made of brass (often silver-plated), tin, and a pot metal of a pewter-type substance, often decayed or became loose from the glass vessel. Often the lids were thrown away. Replaced metal tops are commonplace. While the original tops are preferred, collectors of syrup jugs do not object to the replaced tops. The tops appear in two different shapes—a dome lid and a "duck bull" lid. In replacing a syrup lid, it is most desirable to use the style which was original to the syrup. Replaced syrup lids do not affect the price of the jug.

The three basic jug shapes are bulbous, oval and cylindrical. The SPANISH LACE syrup (Fig. 13) is the only jug which originally came with a reeded handle. All other Victorian cranberry opalescent syrups have a plain (not reeded) handle.

There have been many reproductions of the cranberry opalescent syrup. All of the repros (with one exception) have reeded handles. The re-make of the RING NECK STRIPE syrup uses a plain handle. The difference between the new and old is found in the number of rings on the neck of the jug. The old syrup has one ring on the neck, while the reproduction has two rings (see H3, Figs. 289, 290).

The sugar shaker has few reproductions with which to deal. The one which causes most concern is the NINE PANEL mold (Fig. 139). In judging the age of a sugar shaker, remove the metal top. On an old example, the top edge is slightly rounded and often has a rough, lightly chipped rim, where the piece was removed from the blow pipe. Since this rim was covered by the screw top, there was no reason for the manufacturer to polish the rim. However, on the recent L.G. Wright reproductions (made by Fenton), these rims are usually ground flat with a grainy, frosted appearance.

Chips under the metal lid do not hurt the value of the sugar shaker. Replaced or reproduction lids are not objectionable to most collectors. However, in order to receive the best price for an old sugar shaker, it should be correctly lidded.

To the best of my knowledge, there are no reproductions in cranberry opalescent salt and pepper shakers. The Fenton Art Glass Company produced a "Baby Coinspot" salt shaker (Fig. 325), but it is an original shape and not a reproduction of any old example.

In judging the age of a salt shaker, use the same methods as in determining the authenticity of a sugar shaker. They were both blown and finished in the same manner.

There are no reproduction cranberry opalescent toothpick holders. In fact there are few old cranberry opalescent toothpicks available for today's collectors. Toothpicks in this color are scarce, and the demand so high, that prices are relatively expensive.

THE INFLUENCE OF HARRY NORTHWOOD

No single individual was more responsible for the production of blown opalescent pattern glass in America than the inimitable and ubiquitous Harry Northwood. During his illustrious career as an engraver, designer, chemist, color master, and glass businessman, he personally helped develop the market for "fancy glass" or "Venetian" ware (as this ware was sometimes called in early trade journals) in this country. He was influenced himself, as were others, by his father, the famed John Northwood, and by his years as a young apprentice in Stourbridge, England.

Mr. Northwood's introduction of opalescent blown glassware can be substantiated somewhat by this interesting report from a 1908 trade journal. Take special note of the last sentence.

8/1908 American Pottery Gazette

WELL! Well! And whom have we here? Why yes, of course, Harry Northwood; known wherever glass is sold—and then some! When they want something in colored glass that they never had before, never heard of, that in their own hearts they don't believe exists, they mention it to Harry and then at the next annual showing at Pittsburgh there will be Harry with the goods. And he will have it with a name of his own tacked on to it, too, that will make some of them blink once or twice as well.

*What a thing it is to be famous. Here we have a man who likes nothing better than to do just as he wants to do, and they make him unheard of colors in glass instead. Nevertheless and alas! to quote the novelists, Harry prospers on hard work. He comes from a famous family of glassworkers in England, his father, John Northwood, who death occurred only a few years ago, having already been referred to in these columns as one of the men who made Stourbridge's famous glass an actuality. When Harry came over here in the early eighties, a strapping young fellow in the twenties, he started in to work in Wheeling, W. Va., in one of the old time glass factories. Of course he had to make some colored glass. Just couldn't help it. **They hadn't seen before anything like the opalescent glass he made** for them and his reputation was made from then on.*

A list of the companies for whom Mr. Northwood worked, including four which carried his name, takes up most of the list of manufacturers of blown opalescent in America. Many of the others on the list are firms which remained in operation after Mr. Northwood left the helm, or were established by individuals who worked under Mr. Northwood during their own early careers.

The companies for which Mr. Northwood worked, or those which he personally managed or was part-owner of, are:

HOBBS, BROCKUNIER & CO., Wheeling, W. Va.
LA BELLE GLASS WORKS, Bridgeport, Ohio
PHOENIX GLASS COMPANY, Monaca , Pa.
BUCKEYE GLASS COMPANY, Martin's Ferry, Ohio
NORTHWOOD GLASS COMPANY, Martin's Ferry, Ohio
THE NORTHWOOD GLASS COMPANY, Ellwood City, Pa.
THE NORTHWOOD COMPANY, Indiana, Pa.
NATIONAL GLASS COMPANY—NORTHWOOD GLASS WORKS, Indiana, Pa.
H. NORTHWOOD & COMPANY, Wheeling, W. Va.

Those firms which were started by individuals formerly under Northwood's influence or guidance, which produced blown opalescent tableware, include:

DUGAN GLASS COMPANY, Indiana, Pa.
BEAUMONT GLASS COMPANY, Martin's Ferry, Oh.
JEFFERSON GLASS COMPANY, Steubenville, Oh.
BASTOW GLASS CO., Coudersport, Pa.
FENTON ART GLASS COMPANY, Williamstown, W. Va.
WEST VIRGINIA GLASS MANUFACTURING CO., Martin's Ferry, Oh.

All of the above firms were established by gentlemen who were either related to Northwood by blood or marriage, worked under Northwood at one of his own factories, or who employed him at one time to produce opalescent glass at one of their former factories.

Thus, there is no doubt that Harry Northwood was singly responsible for the many factories competing for their share of the limited market for blown opalescent ware. No company could profit from production of this glass alone, and most firms above also produced some lines of pressed glass. Mr. Northwood's career in America began at the factory of Hobbs, Brockunier & Co. at Wheeling, and when this plant was shut down in 1893 by the U.S. Glass Company, the talent-heavy personnel from Hobbs dispersed to other factories, to continue the tradition of blown opalescent glassware. Thus, his influence at the last three factories listed above may not have been "direct", but it most certainly was indirect, if for no other reason than their attempts to create competitive lines for those being made by his factories at Ellwood City and Indiana, Pa. This book can be considered something of a preview for my upcoming trilogy on Northwood Glass, but Mr. Northwood's other contributions to American glass are so diversified, that this Book 9 would be a mere chapter in this famous man's career.

Today, the tradition of blown opalescent glassware continues directly due to the Northwood heritage. The gorgeous hand-made opalescent glass produced by the Fenton Art Glass Co., a factory established by one of Northwood's former managers, has the color, the quality and the sumptuous warmth of the original glass introduced by Mr. Northwood more than a century ago.

NORTHWOOD BIOGRAPHY

Harry Northwood was born at Wordsley, England, on June 30, 1860, the son of John and Elizabeth (Duggins) Northwood, both of whom were born in Staffordshire. He came of a family that had been associated with the manufacturing of glass in England for many generations. His father was actively concerned in the practical manufacturing of glass, being an artist in cameo glass, renowned for such masterpieces known as "The Birmingham Vase," "The Dennis Vase" and also an exact copy of the famous "Portland Vase," considered to be the greatest work of art in glass reproduction since the Roman era.

Harry Northwood received his early education training in schools of Stourbridge, Worcestershire, England, the center of the glass industry in that country. He began an apprenticeship to the trade of glassworker when he was 14 years of age, and received especially careful instruction under his distinguished father. His early training in all the details of glass manufacturing fortified him for his future management of the many enterprises with which he was so prominently connected.

In 1881, at the tender age of 21, Mr. Northwood severed the ties that bound him to home and native land and came to America. He made Wheeling his destination and accepted employment as a designer and etcher for the firm of Hobbs, Brockunier & Co. On May 27, 1882, he married Miss Clara Elizabeth Beaumont, of Handsworth, Staffordshire, England, to whom two children were born, a son, H. Clarence Northwood, and a daughter, who became Mrs. H. W. Robb. From about 1883 to 1887 Mr. Northwood was associated off and on, with the LaBelle Glass Works at Bridgeport, Oh., and thereafter he was vice-president and general manager of the Northwood Glass Co., at Martin's Ferry, until 1892, when the base of operation was transferred to Ellwood City, Pa., where he continued the incumbent of the same official positions, under the original corporate title of the company, until 1896. Thereafter he was managing partner of the Northwood Co. at Indiana, Pa., until 1899, when he returned to his native country and assumed the position of manager of the London office of the National Glass Co. In 1901 he returned to the United States and soon afterward effected the organization of the H. Northwood & Co., of Wheeling.

He died in February, 1919, but the firm carrying his name continued on until 1924 under the direction of the secretary-treasurer Dent A. Taylor.

Mr. Northwood was an authority in regards to all details of the manufacturing of glassware, in connection with which he invested and successfully introduced various original methods and devices. He held many patents for the production and decoration of glass and many of the glass colors he introduced were copied by competitors with limited success. He was one of the first pressed glass manufacturers to introduce a mark, the Northwood script signature (first used at his Indiana, Pa. factory in 1899-1900) and the popular N-in-a-circle trademark used at Wheeling after 1905. His opalescent, custard and carnival glass is eagerly sought by collectors today.

NORTHWOOD OPALESCENT IN TRADE QUOTES

The attribution and dating of Northwood patterns and molds is a fascinating study in itself. It involves concentration on many details, including colors, shapes, finials, and comparing this field information to trade journal material. Glass industry trade journals help us to definitely date the introduction of certain patterns and molds. The ROYAL IVY pattern was introduced in 1890, and the molds were moved to the new factory, retooled and used for the DAISY & FERN (No. 91?) and PARIAN SWIRL (No. 183?) patterns in 1895. The molds were then moved to Indiana, Pa. and retooled to form the APPLE BLOSSOM pattern. The slight increase in sizes on each of these patterns witnesses the widening depth of the mold as new details are carved into the mold. The same is true of the LEAF UMBRELLA (1889), retooled to form JEWEL (1891) and then again to form QUILTED PHLOX (circa 1896-1903). The No. 245 RIBBED PILLAR (1889) was retooled to form the larger No. 182 PANELLED SPRIG (1895). These last four patterns mentioned can also be found as shape molds for opalescent SWIRL and LATTICE designs.

Studying the trade journals for clues to identify the blown opalescent patterns made by Northwood's various companies and the factories for which he worked can sometimes prove frustrating. These lines were almost never advertised with illustrations, and descriptions are almost non-existant. Almost all opalescent lines were listed by number, and even these prove sometimes to be unreliable, as the journal reporters worked from notes and sometimes these notes became confusing when transferred to their printed reviews. For instance, a June, 1891 report lists Northwood's No. 285 as the No. 385 in the following month's report. Which is correct, No. 285 or 385? Sometimes providing an answer is nothing more than an educated deduction. Could one line be in rubina (formerly called HOBBS OPTIC) and the other be the cased Vasa Murrhina color (PRIMA DONNA)?

The "sea shell" ware is probably the blown glass with applied rigaree which we tend to call Stourbridge glass when found today. P.O., F.O., and B.O. were used to describe pink opalescent, flint opalescent and blue opalescent. The old term for "cranberry" was ruby. The numbers with question marks (?) indicate a possible error, either typographically in the journal or by the confused reporter.

EARLY NORTHWOOD LINES
1888-1897

YEAR	LINE NO.	DESCRIPTION
2/1888	—	Diamond, rib, spot, etc., satin finish
7/1888	206	Complete new line of blown fancy tableware
7/1888	244	Complete new line of blown fancy tableware
1/1889	245	RIBBED PILLAR (NORTHWOOD PLEAT)
7/1889	263	LEAF UMBRELLA
7/1889	260	Lemonade set in p.o., f.o., b.o. (unknown)
7/1889	248	Ruby and Crystal crackled
2/1890	273	Crystal sea shell ware in epergnes, vases, water bottles, round and heart-shaped bonbons
2/1890	274	Caster sets, engraved crystal and ruby
2/1890	272	Opalescent salads, cruets, salt/peppers (unknown)
2/1890	264	Bowls and nappies, crackled crystal and ruby
2/1890	275	Plain ruby jugs and tumblers
7/1890	—	AURORA (see No. 285 below)
7/1890	287	ROYAL IVY
1/1891	317	JEWEL ("Threaded Rubina Swirl")
1/1891	315	ROYAL OAK
1/1891	—	Three new opalescent jugs with tumblers and lemonade sets
6/1891	285	Ruby flash etched (stork) and flower pattern
7/1891	385	Same as above, possibly in vasa murrhina
7/1891	333	ROYAL SILVER (LEAF MOLD in vasa murrhina)
7/1891	333	ROYAL ONYX (LEAF MOLD in spatter)
1/1892	34 (?)	ROYAL ART in two effects, bright and satin
1/1892	343	A full line (reference to No. 34 above?)
1/1892	339	Spangled ware in water sets, odds and ends, berry bowls and other novelties
8/1892	—	Ellwood GRANITE WARE (speckled finish); night lamps in ivory (custard) and blue
1/1893	—	Two Tea (table) sets in green and ruby (cranberry), baskets, jugs, tankards, cruets, syrups, vases in colors and color combinations
3/1893	403	Sets in green and ruby
3/1893	404	Lamps in canary, blue and ruby (probably opales)
1/1895	91 (?)	Full line of opalescent—f.o., p.o., b.o. (DAISY AND FERN in Parian Swirl molds?)
1/1895	182	Crystal and ruby flash [PANELLED SPRIG] with gold and enamel decoration
8/1895	183	New line, ruby or crystal decorated (PARIAN SWIRL?)
8/1895	204	New line in crystal
8/1895	205	Pint and quart jugs, in all opalescent colors
8/1895	600	Lamp in five sizes and hand-lamp, plain or decorated crystal
8/1895	502-504	Pressed jellies in fancy shapes
1/1896	215	Opal tableware with delft decoration
1/1896	217	Full line with reverse central spot pattern (POLKA DOT in FANCY FANS mold)
3/1896	—	Nos. 205, 319, 217, 187, 360 and other lemonade sets advertised available at Indiana, Pa. plant
2/1897	—	New things being added in blown opal, blue, ruby and color combinations

Perhaps the must difficult matchup is determining if one the first three descriptions above refers to the RIBBED OPAL LATTICE and RIBBED COINSPOT tableware patterns. The second and third listing, although not naming opalescent ware specifically, refer to complete lines. Either No. 206 or 244 could be RIBBED OPAL LATTICE. What would the other line be? At first I thought it had to be the CHRYSANTHEMUM SWIRL, which is known in satin or shiny finish. It was offered in Butler Bros. catalogues in 1889-90. We know REVERSE SWIRL was made by Buckeye. Why would Buckeye make such a similar line at the same time? Both lines come in speckled finish, without opalescent finish. Northwood made some of his glass in a speckled finish (PANELLED SPRIG). Both lines also come in satin finish. One important fact denotes separate manufacturers. REVERSE SWIRL was made in yellow opalescent. There is no yellow opalescent in CHRYSANTHEMUM SWIRL. No canary color is mentioned in Northwood displays until after the firm moved to Ellwood City, and then only in lamps. The Fig. 190 SWIRL and Northwood's JEWEL ("Threaded Rubina Swirl") pattern are known in an unusual tall bar bottle, a rare shape. A January, 1891 journal mentions, "The company have another new departure in a line of bar bottles which they expect big things from." And finally, two trade quotes, one from this same 1888 journal, clearly mention straw jars in Northwood's displays. There are only two of these known in opalescent glass patterns, and CHRYSANTHEMUM SWIRL is one of them. The other known straw jar, Fig. 246 in this book, matches either a Beaumont or Hobbs shape mold.

However, strong evidence points elsewhere to the origins of CHRYSANTHEMUM SWIRL. The answer seems to involve John F. Miller, who worked at Buckeye and then opened his own company at Anderson, Ind. (American Glass Co.) in 1889. He held a patent for opalescent glass with stripes, and possibly introduced CHRYSANTHEMUM SWIRL at his new Indiana factory. See the history of this company for further information.

After Northwood moved from Ellwood City to Indiana, Pa., in February, 1896, apparently taking some molds with him, the use of pattern names, instead of numbers, became standard. APPLE BLOSSOM, CRYSTAL QUEEN, KLONDYKE (Fluted Scrolls), ALASKA, LOUIS XV, OPALINE BROCADE (Spanish Lace), VENETIAN (Utopia Optic), INTAGLIO, PAGODA (Inverted Fan & Feather), and NAUTILUS (Argonaut Shell) were all designed by Northwood or his associates before he sold out to National and went to London as their European representative.

Some of the more important trade quotes are reprinted next in order that you may also distinguish clues from the descriptions. Only quotes involving blown opalescent are reprinted. The larger Northwood books will detail the other numbered lines above.

IMPORTANT TRADE QUOTES:

2/9/1888 P&GR

Capt. S. C. Dunlevy has a beautiful exhibit of the goods manufactured by the Northwood Glass Co., of Martin's Ferry , at the Monongahela House. They are chiefly blown lead goods and comprise tableware, water sets, flower holders, molasses cans, shades, gas globes, water bottles, finger bowls, hall globes, tumblers, casters, oil bottles, salt, pepper and oil cruets, and a general line of fancy glassware. The colors are most exquisite and include effects in satin finish, diamond, rib, spot, etc. This company's works are now in operation.

7/19/1888 P&GR

Captain Seymour C. Dunlevy is staying at Room 137 and represents the NORTHWOOD GLASS CO., of Martin's Ferry, Ohio. This concern has achieved much celebrity in the manufacture of fine blown tableware, fancy goods, globes, shades, fine colors, and effects, and their products are without a peer in the market. H. Helling is president of the company; A. W. Kerr, secretary; H. Floto, treasurer; Harry Northwood, manager, and Captain S. C. Dunlevy, general salesman. Their specialty as noted above, is artistic glass ware in fine colors and of a superior quality of metal, and includes a large diversity of articles. They have now ready two complete new lines of blown fancy tableware, Nos. 206 and 244. They have a fine selection of vases, jugs, tankards, casters, fancy straw jars, bitter bottles, water sets, and other things too numerous to specify. The number of shapes is practically without limit and the same may be said of the colors and combinations of color all of which are extrememly beautiful, rich and effective. They make both flint and lime glass at this establishment, all of the best kind. No mere written description can give anything like a correct idea of the elegance and attractiveness of these goods; they must be seen and judged for themselves.

7/25/1889 P & GR

THE NORTHWOOD GLASS CO., of Martin's Ferry, has a large line of samples at Room No. 121, in charge of Mr. B. Long, who has already booked some good orders. Mr. Long has a full line of everything made by the Northwood, consisting of tableware, dome shades and novelties. No. 263 [LEAF UMBRELLA], the new fall line of tableware made in rose du Barry, ruby, and crystal, is the finest ever made by the Northwood, which is saying a great deal. Tooth picks are also made in this line. All the dealers who have seen the new line express themselves as highly pleased with it. A new line of lemonade sets in P.O., F.O. and B.O. have been brought out. The number is 260. A nut bowl in ruby, with marble edges, is ready for the fall trade, also other novelties. The straw jars, P.O., F.O. and B.O. and in No. 245, are the finest in the market. They have fifteen different water sets. In 14 inch dome shades, they exhibit the largest variety of colors in the market and new ones are constantly added. The latest is No. 248 in ruby and crystal crackled. They have a large assortment [sic] of caseters [sic], with 2,3 and 4 bottles, and hand made bowls for fruit, nuts, roses and oranges. The rose bowl in royal ruby is great. Their royal ruby line, the finest they make, and others all introduced within a year, are going off very well.

2/13/1890 P&GR

Martin's Ferry — THE NORTHWOOD GLASS WORKS is running every day and doing well. This enterprise has a very large line of novelties for the spring trade, which are selling like hot cakes. No. 273, made in crystal sea shell ware and consisting of epergnes, flower vases, water bottles, plates and round and heart shaped bonbons is very artistic [probably blown cranberry with crystal applied rigaree similar to rows of sea shells, previously thought to be English only]. *Pretty casters and bottles are made in crystal engraved* and ruby, the number of which is 274. Opalescent salads, oils and vinegars, salts and peppers, the number of which is 272, are goods that are bound to become popular. Brownies, Greenaways and tumblers in etched are very pretty, also their crystal engraved pitchers and tumblers in both lines of crystal and ruby, with tumblers to match. The No. 264 bowls and nappies in crackled, crystal and ruby; No. 267 twist salts and peppers, in blue, canary and ruby; No. 275 plain ruby jugs and tumblers; No. 280 crystal engraved decanters, and No. 281 crystal jugs and tumblers, engraved and cut, are also among the new spring ware. These goods are all new and a credit to the Northwood. Some of them have already become popular. Mr. Harry Northwood, the efficient manager, is to be complimented for bringing out such a fine lione of spring goods.

8/14/95 CG&L

MARTIN'S FERRY, O. [should be ELLWOOD CITY] — *The Northwood Glass Co. have ready for the trade many new and strikingly handsome goods which must prove great trade promoters. Among these are two new lines: No. 183, decorated in ruby or crystal, and No. 204 in crystal. No. 271 is a very pretty decorated wine set in crystal. No. 197 is a set done up in the new process etching. There are three new lines of flower vases in crystal, from 6 to 20 inches high. No. 197 is a tankard in crystal, decorated or etched. No. 211 is a paste mold jug with crimped top, decorated or etched. No. 500 is a new flower vase. Nos. 502, 503 and 504 are jellies, pressed and finished in fancy shapes.* **No. 205 is a pint and quart jug, made in all opalescent colors.** *Then there are an endless variety of etchings and decorations on lemonade sets to suit cottage or palace. In the way of lamps No. 600 is a new one made in five sizes and hand lamp, either in plain or crystal or with decorations, all very handsome.*

1/15/96 CG&L

The most individual and artistic colored glassware on exhibit this season will be found in room 156, and consists of two new sets of tableware varied in color and artistic decoration with a breadth and finish certain to suit the widest diversity of taste. The No. 215 is a graceful set of opal tableware, decorated in blue, after the famous delft porcelain, which has enjoyed such a large run during the past year, and been favored with the patronage of the most cultured and fashionable metropolitan buyers. The characteristic feature about the set is that the hand-painted decors are originals, not mass reproductions or imitations laid on with a stencil, and which the country is to be flooded and overgorged, but no two pieces are decorated alike, and there is an individuality, distinctness, and separate artistic effort and effect in each piece of the same set, which stales not upon the eye, because of infinite variety and distinctiveness of design. The No. 217 [Opalescent POLKA DOT in FANCY FANS mold] *is also a full line, very handsome in form,* **the pattern being a reversed central colored spot, shown throughout the casing, and comes in flint, ruby and blue opalescent,** *making one of the finest color combinations ever turned out by the Northwood firm. The decorated, needle etched flint lemonade sets, vases and colored novelties, lamps, rose bowls, etc., make an exhibit of artistic colored glassware which delights the eye, and increases one's respect for the craft, art touch and inventive mind which fashioned and evolved these gems of the glassmakers' art.*

3/11/96

[Advertisement announces]

NORTHWOOD GLASS CO.
Indiana, PA.
Now ready with a Fine Line of
Colored and Opal Decorated Glassware
... Your orders solicited for No. 205, No. 319, No. 217, No. 187, No. 360 and other Lemonade Sets. A new line of opal decorated lamps will be ready May 1.

11/15/1902 CG&L

There is a real novelty in a lemonade set shown here from the Northwood factory. This set and some new molasses cans are among the newest things on the display tables of Frank Miller, the New York representative of H. Northwood & Co. The lemonade set referred to has a jug of graceful shape, but is is the decoration which at once attracts the eye. **Its flower and foliage seem to stick right out, although the relief is not high** [OPAL POINSETTIA]. *The effect is secured by the opalescent tint of the relief, which upon the various backgrounds of canary, flint, blue and pink, is most striking. It is certainly a novelty and shows that Mr. Northwood knows how to produce original effects. Still, he usually did do that. The molasses cans have nothing new in the shapes, but they are revivals of one of the best selling shapes we ever had* [the tall tapered syrup], *and, made as the Northwood factory is making them, in dainty colors, why shouldn't they sell better than ever they did?*

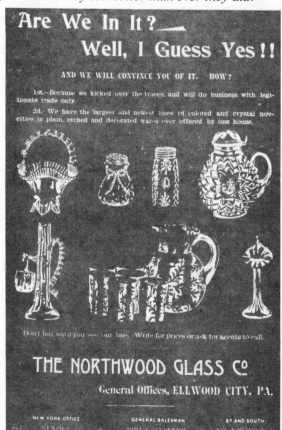

One of the few known illustrated advertisements from The Northwood Glass Co. at Ellwood City, Pa. This 1895 ad pictures a lemonade set in DAISY & FERN (with six tumblers). Also pictured are three blown glass items reminiscent of English off-hand art glass.

Reference Key

AG—Various authors, *American Glass from the Pages of ANTIQUES* (magazine article reprints)

BB—Butler Brothers catalogues

BMG—E. McCamly Belknap's *Milk Glass*

BRS—Richard Carter Barret's *Popular American Ruby-Stained Pattern Glass* (out-of-print)

BTG1 & 2—Fred Bickenheuser's *Tiffin Glassmasters*, Books 1 & 2

Barnett—Jerry Barnett's *Paden City—The Color Company*

Batty—Bob Batty's *A Complete Guide to Pressed Glass*

Bennett—Reprint of 1903 Cambridge catalogue by Harold & Judy Bennett

Bishop—James W. Bishop's *The Glass Industry of Allegany County, Maryland*

Bond—Marcelle Bond's *The Beauty of Albany Glass* (out-of-print)

Bones—Frances Bones' *The Book of Duncan Glass*

Boultinghouse—Mark Boultinghouse's *Art and Colored Glass Toothpick Holders* (out-of-print)

C & GJ—*Crockery & Glass Journal* (early trade journal)

CGC1—Reprint of 1930-34 Cambridge catalogues by National Cambridge Collectors, Inc.

CGC2—Reprint of 1949-53 Cambridge catalogues by NCC, Inc.

CGW—Marion Quintin-Baxendale's *Carnival Glass Worldwide*

CMG—Microfilm research files of unpublished material at the Corning Museum of Glass

Edwards—Bill Edwards' *The Standard Encyclopedia of Carnival Glass* and price guide

FB—Personal research files of Fred Bickenheuser

FGM—Research archive of the Fenton Glass Museum

F1 & F2—William Heacock's *Fenton Glass—The First 25 Years* and *Fenton Glass—The Second 25 Years*

Ferson—Regis & Mary Ferson's *Yesterday's Milk Glass Today*

Forsythe—Ruth Forsythe's *Made in Czechoslovakia*

GC—*The Glass Collector*, research quarterly

GDS—Reprint of Geo. Duncan & Sons catalogue, circa 1890 (George A. Fogg)

GR—*Glass Review* magazine, published ten times yearly, Barbara Shaeffer, editor

GR—*Glass Review* magazine, published twelve times yearly, Barbara Shaeffer, editor

Godden—Geoffrey A. Godden's *Antique Glass & China* (England)

H1-H6—Heacock series *The Encyclopedia of Victorian Colored Pattern Glass*, Books 1-6

Hammond CC—Dorothy Hammond's *Confusing Collectibles* (1979 edition)

HAR NOR—Marion Hartung's *Northwood Pattern Glass*

HAR OP—Marion Hartung's *Opalescent Pattern Glass*

Herrick—Ruth Herrick's *Greentown Glass* (out-of-print)

IG—Margaret & Douglas Archer's *Imperial Glass* catalogue reprint

Innes—Lowell Innes' *Pittsburgh Glass, 1797-1891*

JSB—J. Stanley Brothers' *Thumbnail Sketches* (out-of-print)

James—Margaret James' *Black Glass*

K1-K8—Minnie Kamm's series on pattern glass, Books 1-8

Knittle—Rhea Mansfield Knittle's *Early American Glass*

Krause—Gail Krause's *The Years of Duncan*

Krause DG—Gail Krause's *Duncan Glass*

LPG—Ruth Webb Lee's *Early American Pressed Glass*

LSG—Ruth Webb Lee's *Sandwich Glass*

LVG—Ruth Webb Lee's *Victorian Glass*

Lattimore—Colin Lattimore's *English 19th-Century Press-moulded Glass*

Lafferty TP—James R. Lafferty, Sr.'s *The Phoenix* (Phoenix Glass Company)

Lafferty FI—James R. Lafferty, Sr.'s *Fry Insights*

Lagerberg 1-4—Ted & Vi Lagerberg's series of four books on *Collectible Glass*

Lechler—Doris Lechler & Virginia O'Neill's *Children's Glass Dishes*

Lechler 2—Doris Lechler's *Children's Glass Dishes, China and Furniture*

Lindsey—Bessie Lindsey's *American Historical Glass*

Lucas—Robert I. Lucas' *Tarentum Pattern Glass* (limited edition)

McCain—Mollie Helen McCains *The Collector's Encyclopedia of Pattern Glass*

MH1-MH10—Marion Hartung's series on Carnival Glass, Books 1-10

MD OG—S. T. Millard's *Opaque Glass*

M/W—Helen McKearin and Kenneth Wilson's *American Bottles and Flasks and Their Ancestry*

MVG—*M'Kee Victorian Glass* (Corning Museum catalogue reprints)

Measell—James Measell's *Greentown Glass*

Metz 1 & 2—Alice Metz's two books on *Early American Pattern Glass*

Millard 1 & 2 (or Md1 & Md2)—S. T. Millard's *Goblets 1* and *Goblets 2*

Morris—Barbara Morris' *Victorian Table Glass & Ornaments* (England)

NMG 1 & 2—Everett & Addie Miller's two books on New Martinsville Glass Co.

Newman—Harold Newman's *An Illustrated Dictionary of Glass*

1000 TPH—William Heacock's *1000 Toothpick Holders*

OPG—William Heacock's *Old Pattern Glass—According to Heacock*

OS—Heacock & Johnsons' *5000 Open Salts*

PG—Pyne Press' *Pennsylvania Glassware 1870-1904*

PGP 1-6—Set of six *Pattern Glass Previews*, 1981 newsletter

Pears—Thomas C. Pears III *Bakewell, Pears & Co. Glass Catalogue*

Pet Pat—Arthur Peterson's *Glass Patents & Patterns*

Pet Sal—Arthur Peterson's *Glass Salt Shakers*

Pet TM—Arthur G. Peterson's *400 Trademarks on Glass*

Revi—A. C. Revi's *American Pressed Glass & Figure Bottles* (out-of-print)

Revi AANG—A. C. Revi's *American Art Nouveau Glass*

Revi NCG—A. C. Revi's *Nineteenth Century Glass*

RP1-4—Rose Presznick's series of 4 books on *Carnival and Iridescent Glass* (out-of-print)

RU/TP—William Heacock's *Rare & Unlisted Toothpick Holders*

Smith FPG—Don Smith's *Findlay Pattern Glass* (out-of-print)

Spillman—Jane Shadel Spillman's *American & European Pressed Glass* (Corning Museum)

Stevens CG—Gerald Stevens' *Canadian Glass—1825-1925*

Stevens GIC—Gerald Stevens' *Glass in Canada*

Stout—Sandra Stout's *The Complete Book of McKee Glass*

Stout 1-3—Sandra Stout's three color books on Depression Glass

SWA—*Antiques—From the Pages of Spinning Wheel Magazine* (article reprints)

Taylor—Ardelle Taylor's *Colored Glass Syrups and Sugar Shakers* (out-of-print)

Thuro—Catherine M. V. Thuro's *Oil Lamps—The Kerosene Era in North America*

Thuro2—Catherine M. V. Thuro's *Oil Lamps 2—Glass Kerosene Lamps*

Toulouse—Julian H. Toulouse's *Bottle Makers and Their Marks*

U1 & U2—Doris & Peter Unitt's two books on *American & Canadian Goblets*

UCG—Doris & Peter Unitt's *Treasury of Canadian Glass*

U/W—Peter Unitt & Anne Worrall's *Canadian Handbook of Pressed Glass Tableware*

VR—Steven Van Rensselaer's *Early American Bottles and Flasks*

Vogel 1-4—Clarence Vogel's set of four A. H. Heisey and Co. catalogue reprints

WDG 1 & 2—Hazel Weatherman's two books on colored glass of the Depression era

WFG—Hazel Weatherman's *Fostoria—Its First 50 Years*

WPT2—Hazel Weatherman's 1982 *Supplement & Price Trends* to her WDG2

WSC—Westmoreland Specialty Co. 1912 catalogue

Welker 1 & 2—Mary, Lyle & Lynn Welker's reprints of Cambridge Glass catalogues

Whitmyer—Margaret & Kenn Whitmyer's *Children's Dishes*

The Manufacturers

PHOENIX GLASS COMPANY
Monaca, Pa.
(1880-present)

The company was founded in 1880 in Phillipsburg, Pa. (which became Monaca in 1892). Andrew Howard was the founder and President, and William I. Miller was secretary-treasurer. At first the firm made only chimneys and reflectors, with the capacity of only one ten-pot furnace. In 1882 they added gas shades to their line, as well as lamp globes. In Feb., 1884, the plant burned down. To keep in operation, the Phoenix then may have bought an old abandoned chimney works formerly operated by Doyle, Sons & C., at Phillipsburg. This Doyle chimney factory had no association with the Doyle tableware factory in Pittsburgh. However, a 1946 trade journal, in a brief history of the Phoenix firm, clearly stated the Doyle factory was at Pittsburgh.

When Phoenix's main plant was reconstructed, the "Doyle" factory became known as "Plant No. 3" (Phoenix had a second 14-pot factory making lighting ware in Washington, Pa. from 1902-14). Lafferty's *The Phoenix* clearly indicates that the No. 3 factory was in Monaca (formerly Phillipsburg). My Phoenix files indicate that this plant was originally used for making incandescent bulbs, and was still operating in 1946. In 1885 the Phoenix plant at Phillipsburg was rebuilt with a second furnace added. The company reorganized in 1891. In 1893 another fire destroyed the main plant. Phoenix then leased the old Dithridge plant at New Brighton, Pa. The main plant was rebuilt again. The Washington, Pa. factory was sold in 1902. The main focus of production since 1890 has been in the field of lighting ware.

This brief and confusing history, taken from trade journal records, helps dispel some of the mystery of the so-called "Doyle takeover" reported by Kamm, Innes, Revi and others. Both Doyle and Phoenix suffered from a number of fires, but Phoenix purchased an old abandoned "Doyle" factory, not interest in the firm itself.

The Phoenix factory originally made chimneys, but soon branched into gas shades, and in 1883, in a surprising change of direction, entered the competitive field of art glass. This was made possible through the acquisition of Joseph Webb, nephew of the famed English glassmaker Thomas Webb, as plant superintendent. An October, 1883, trade journal describes Phoenix lines in crackled ware. The following month Phoenix sold a set of 17 "hob-nail" molds to the Elson Glass Co. of Martin's Ferry, Oh. These may have been for a line of tableware which today would be identified as one of the many variants of DAISY AND BUTTON. This sale may have been instigated by the changeover to art glass production. However, see *PGA, pp. 362-363* for a "Hobnail" design made by Elson. The industry term for this type ware was usually "Dew Drop".

The best, and most important, description of much of Phoenix's line from this period appeared the following year, on Christmas Day, 1884. It stated:

The extensive glass works of the Phoenix Glass Co. are situated at Phillipsburg, on the Pittsburgh, & Lake Erie railroad, about 27 miles from Pittsburgh, in which latter place they have their sample rooms and general offices. These works are newly built, having been entirely reconstructed after the great fire which completely destroyed them early last spring.

*. . . Formerly this firm worked chiefly on chimneys, afterward they commenced on shades, and still later on colored glassware, which is at present their most notable product. They make chimneys yet, however, and the finest lines of decorated shades in the country, but in colored glassware they have achieved a triumph never before consummated in the land. The variety of shapes, shades and colors in this ware they have on exhibition at their factory is perfectly bewildering, and altogether impossible to describe. They have table sets, pitchers of all sizes and descriptions, ice cream sets, finger bowls, water sets, berry sets, and a host of other miscellaneous wares. The diversity of colors in itself is not so remarkable as the fine shading of one color into another and the different shades in the one and the same article, which shows a different color as one changes its position in relation to the light. Some of the articles have a body of one color and are **plated or cased inside with a different color** and the effect is very fine. Also on pieces cased outside the colored part is cut away by machinery in any desired pattern and leaves the crystal to be seen beneath, forming a crystal design on colored ground. Among the colors are **carnelian, topazine, amberine, azurine, all shades of opalescent, such as flint, spotted, blue, crystal, canary, pink, etc., rose, blue, green, all shades of red, ruby, amber, blue and gold,** and numerous others. They also make kerosene and glass globes and duplex chimneys in all colors and finely engraved, as well as salt and pepper sets, vases and ornamental glass, of every kind. The colors are all brilliant, sparkling and full of life and spirit, if such an expression be permissible, and combinations of shades are here produced that have never before been attempted in this country or Europe.*

Clearly, Mr. Webb influenced the production of art glass and opalescent glass far greater than history heretofore credits. An 1885 trade journal advertises Phoenix as the sole manufacturers of WEBB ART GLASS in America. But he was not alone among the geniuses capable of producing the popular colors and treatments at Phoenix in the 1880's. Another famous glassmaker of English origin, Harry Northwood, was also working at Phoenix in 1885 and early 1886.

To fully understand Northwood's contributions to the colored and art glass production at Phoenix, his whereabouts must be studied. In early 1884, a disastrous flood closed down production at the LaBelle Glass Works in Bridgeport, Ohio. No new glass was made in 1884, with sales being made only from existing stock on hand. In late 1884, as the firm prepared to begin operations again after the flood damage was repaired, another crippling blow hit the area. A devastating strike closed many of the Ohio River valley glass factories for most of the next year. The LaBelle had to reorganize in 1885 and the workers did not return until January of 1886. With no glass being made at LaBelle for almost two full years, the firm certainly could not afford to keep a mold designer working. No mention of Mr. Northwood in trade journals could be found during that period (2/84 to 2/86), but in April of 1885, a patent was filed by John Northwood, famous father of Harry, giving Harry Northwood's address as "Bridgewater, Penn." All rights were assigned by John to Harry. In September of that same year, Harry then sold his rights to this patented crimping device to Phoenix Glass Co., Pittsburgh, Pa. (probably the company office headquarters). That same month the strike at the Ohio River Valley factories was beginning to end, but a reorganized La Belle did not start making glass again until the beginning of 1886. Mr. Northwood returned that year, being back at La Belle in February, 1886. Finally, we know he worked at Phoenix otherwise, as a trade journal report from 1908 lists this firm in his background, and an obituary for Mr. Northwood in 1919 clearly names Phoenix as one of his previous employers.

Phoenix continued to produce art glass until about 1892, when the firm was graduating to cut glass and around 1900 concentrated primarily on lighting ware. Except for a brief period during the 1930's, when the firm produced glass from molds acquired at Co-Operative Flint and Consolidated Lamp & Glass, and during a brief few years in the early 1940's, when Phoenix made a line of Sculptured Artware, this firm remained in the lighting ware field. Today is part of the Anchor Hocking conglomerate.

HOBBS, BROCKUNIER & CO. (1863-1888)
HOBBS GLASS CO. (1888-1891)
U.S. GLASS CO. — Factory H (1891-1893) Wheeling, W. Va.

In April 1845, a glass factory at Wheeling passed into the hands of James B. Barnes and John L. Hobbs, who came to Wheeling from Massachusetts. In 1849 and in 1856 there were changes in the firm that did not have any effect on the operation of the plant. In 1861, when the civil war began, the fires in the furnace were out for six month, many of the men enlisting in the army. In 1863 the firm of Hobbs, Brockunier & Co. was formed, which, with slight changes, operated the plant until 1891. Harry Northwood was their engraver in 1882, and moved to La Belle in 1884. In 1886 the

No. 323 HOBNAIL line, originally called PINEAPPLE, was introduced in pressed and blown glass.

When the charter for Hobbs, Brockunier expired on December 31, 1887, the firm was reorganized in mid-1888 as the Hobbs Glass Co. A strike in early 1888 kept the factory idle for some months during reorganization efforts. At this time, Mr. William Leighton, Jr., one of the co-owners and a glassmaker in his own right, left to associate himself with Dalzell, Gilmore & Leighton at Findlay (where ROSE ONYX was made), and sales manager L. B. Martin left to help organize the new Fostoria Glass Co. at Fostoria, Oh. (where no opalescent was known made). Mr. Nicholas Kopp (later at Consolidated Lamp & Glass, where CRISS-CROSS was made), took charge of production at about this time. Other gentlemen associated with Hobbs, Brockunier (and later Hobbs Glass Co.) were influential in the production of blown opalescent. S.C. Dunlevy, formerly President of La Belle, became Hobbs' manager in 1887 and remained with the firm until the end. Percy Beaumont left in 1888 to join his brother-in-law, Harry Northwood, at his new Martin's Ferry company, but returned to Hobbs in 1890. In 1889, the No. 326 WINDOWS pattern was introduced in the same shape molds as used for their FRANCES WARE SWIRL line. They also produced a No. 328 water set, exact pattern uncertain, in several opalescent colors, including an unusual amber opalescent. The firm was absorbed by the U.S. Glass company and closed in 1893 during a strike by their union workers. The factory remained idle for the next ten years, when it was reopened by none other than the gentleman who started there around 1882, Harry Northwood. A refurbished factory then became H. Northwood & Co.

Thus, we come full circle from the American origins of cranberry opalescent by this and other Northwood-associated firms around 1885-86, to the continuation of its production at Wheeling after 1903.

Existing catalogues reprinted by myself and others help attribute most Hobbs, Brockunier and Hobbs Glass Co. opalescent patterns. The catalogues shown in H6, pp. 49-64 date from 1887 to 1891. Those in H5 date from the U.S. Glass years, circa 1892-93. Those in H2 date from about 1890-91, and includes two lines made later by Beaumont. The opalescent blown patterns made by this firm were copied or closely resemble items and patterns made by others. These include STARS AND STRIPES and SEAWEED (both made later by Beaumont), WINDOWS (copied with larger dots by Buckeye), HOBNAIL (also made by La Belle), SWIRL and STRIPE (both made by several firms).

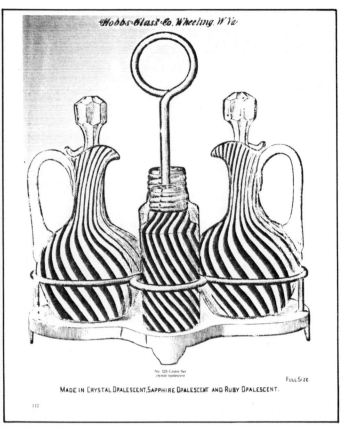

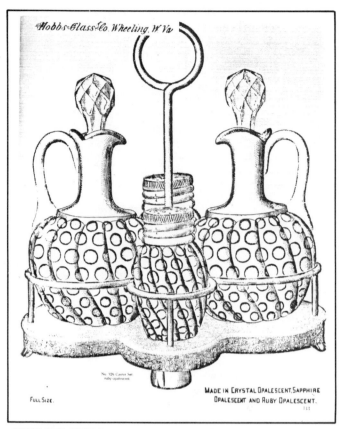

OPAL SWIRL caster set in metal holder from circa 1891 Hobbs Glass Co. catalogue

WINDOWS SWIRL caster set in metal holder from same circa 1891 catalogue

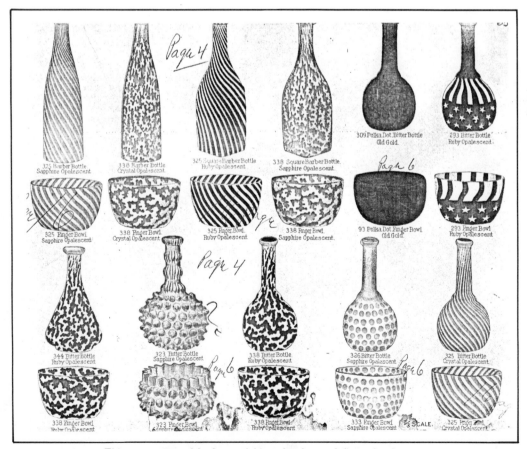

This assortment of barber and bitter bottles, and finger bowls, were reproduced by Beaumont Glass Co. around 1899 (see page 30)

17

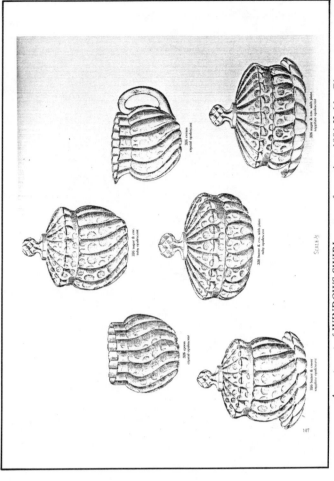

Assortment of WINDOWS SWIRL pattern from circa 1891 Hobbs Glass Co. catalogue

Variety of shapes in HOBBS' SWIRL and OPAL STARS AND STRIPES from same 1891 catalogue. Many of these shapes were copied in 1900

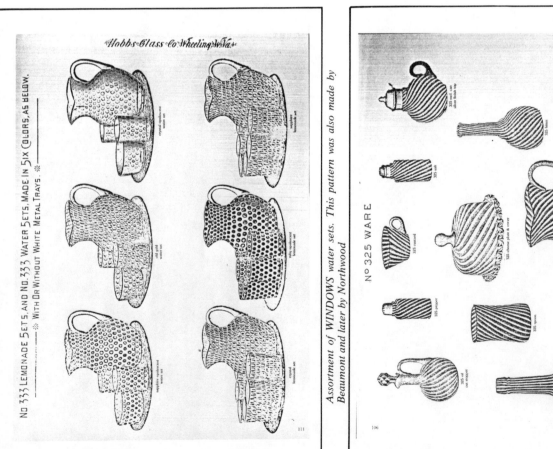

Assortment of WINDOWS water sets. This pattern was also made by Beaumont and later by Northwood

Assortment of No. 325 OPAL SWIRL (HOBB'S SWIRL)

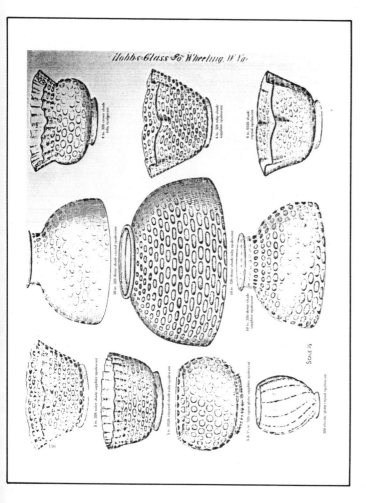

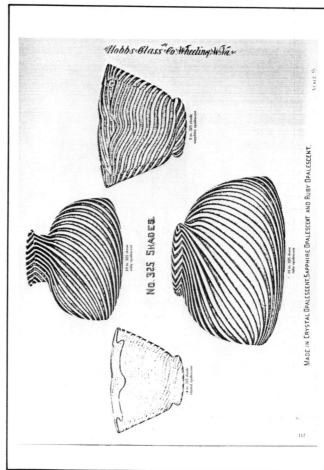

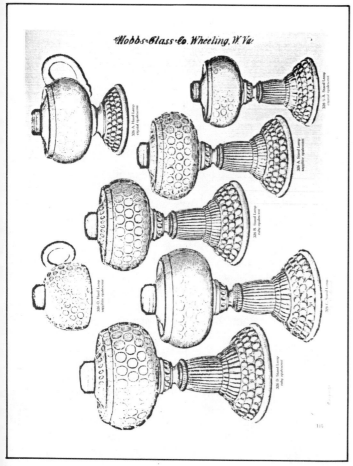

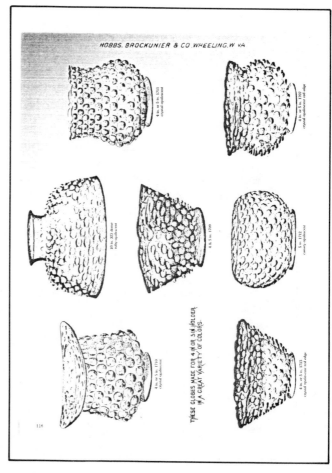

Variety of lamps and shades from 1888 (bottom right) and 1891 catalogues of Hobbs, Brockunier and its successor Hobbs Glass Co.

LA BELLE GLASS CO.
Bridgeport, Ohio (1872-1888)

This company was established in 1872, and at first concentrated on production of pressed tableware. In February, 1884 the firm acquired the services of Harry Northwood from Hobbs, Brockunier & Co. in nearby Wheeling, W. Va., as an engraver, and later as a designer and mold maker. In late 1884, the factory was shut down by a major strike by the workers of the Wheeling area, and Mr. Northwood had to find work elsewhere. He thus relocated to the Phoenix factory, where blown opalescent and art glass was being made at the time. In early 1886, a line of opalescent was being produced at La Belle, with the returning Mr. Northwood in charge of the mold and design department, but the only pattern which can positively be attributed to this firm is the copy of Hobbs' HOBNAIL design. No doubt, other lines in blown opalescent could have been produced here.

In April, 1887 Northwood was wooed by the competing Buckeye Glass Co., of nearby Martin's Ferry, but a week later he returned to LaBelle with a promotion offer. He was sent by the firm to England, accompanied by his wife, to get pointers for new lines. He was no doubt influenced by this trip, leaving in June of 1887. But the La Belle output by Northwood was minimal, as the factory burned down in September of that year, probably before his return. The company leased facilities at a Brilliant, O. factory, while a new La Belle factory was immediately rebuilt, but the financial drain of this new construction caused the firm to enter bankruptcy. It was sold in late 1888 and established as the Crystal Glass Works, with the new factory operating another twenty years under this name. No blown opalescent glass was known made by Crystal.

It appears the Hobbs and La Belle HOBNAIL lines are very difficult to differentiate. The cased colors may be La Belle, based on the trade journal descriptions below. La Belle also probably copied Hobbs' No. 207 SATINA SWIRL design (*H6, p. 56*), the copy being known in several cased colors, but not in opalescent. La Belle probably made some of the items shown in this book which are called "possibly Phoenix", since Mr. Northwood moved from one firm to the other during the glassworkers' strike. I also believe this firm made the "LADY OPAL" toothpick holder (Fig. 217), mugs, tumblers and other drinking vessels in the same plain design (one seen dated 1887). Since this could be Phoenix, I have changed the named from "LaBelle Opal" (*H1, Fig. 197*) to LADY OPAL to prevent confusion in the future.

IMPORTANT JOURNAL QUOTES:
2/18/1886 P&GR

*The La Belle Glass Co., Bridgeport, Ohio, are now in full and successful operation, and able to meet orders punctually. The lines they are now manufacturing include handsome novelties in table and bar ware, lamps, stationers', gas and kerosene goods. In fancy colored ware they are making canary, amber, Rose du Barrie, ivory, blue, topaz, citron, pomona, turquoise, **ruby and opalescent colors**. They are making both lime and lead glass, under the superintendence of Mr. H. Northwood, of Stourbridge, England, a place famous for the production of fine fancy glassware. From present indications the La Belle Co. look for a great run on their new ware, as, though they are in operation only a short time, it is already attracting the attention of the trade.*

They have a fine factory here, with excellent facilities in every way, and are assured of a busy and prosperous season.

8/26/1886 P&GR

*The La Belle Glass Company, of Bridgeport, Ohio, are running one furnace double turn and have out quite a number of new specialties for the fall trade. They are getting out something new in **brilliant colors and combinations** all the time. They have had a very large trade on their new **Dew Drop** set.*

1/27/1887 P&GR

*The La Belle Co.'s new line of opalescent tableware, the **"Dew-drop"**, is simply superb, and those wanting something rich and novel for the spring trade should lose no time in ordering it. This firm have made a marked success in the production of fine colored glass and their latest effort is worthy of their previous successes.*

3/17/1887 P&GR

*The La Belle has just started its second furnace and has about all it can do to fill orders for their new line of **plain and opalescent table ware**, new line of rock crystal, new effects and shapes in globes. The ware made here is hard to beat. A visit to their sample room is a pleasure. It is well filled with artistic novelties in tableware, bar ware, lamps, stationers' gas and kerosene goods, **canary, amber, blue, topaz, rose du Barry, ruby, citron, pomona, ivory, turquoise, allochroite and all opalescent colors**. The outlook is very good.*

BUCKEYE GLASS COMPANY
Martin's Ferry, Oh.
(1878-1896)

This diverse company was founded in 1878 at Martin's Ferry, and was one of the pressed glass tableware factories to introduce color when it came into vogue around 1884. The firm was founded by Henry Helling, a wealthy entrepreneur, who later helped establish the Northwood Glass Company in the same town. Another Buckeye member who was influential in opalescent glass production was John F. Miller, later manager of American Glass Co. (Anderson) and Model Flint Glass Works' (Albany) in Indiana. Much has been written about Buckeye's acquisition of Harry Northwood in April of 1887 from the La Belle Glass Works at nearby Bridgeport. But he was there a mere single week before he was induced back to La Belle with more money and a promotion. However, his influence on a change in production direction at Buckeye is unquestionable, as the firm began production of opalescent and cased art glass colors almost immediately afterward. A trade journal notice from two months later describes opalescent "Dew Drop" (BIG WINDOWS?), "Venetian Threaded" (Opalescent SWIRL?), night lamps, oil cruets, etc. It has also been reported that Northwood shared his expertise with Buckeye while he simultaneously ran his own works in the same town after 1888. This also appears to be an error interpreting a journal notice which, under a Buckeye heading, described that the secretary of the Northwood concern, A.W. Kerr, resigned in 1891 to return to his old position as secretary

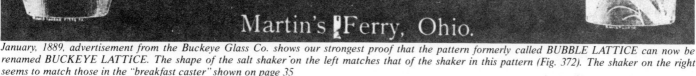

COLORED and OPALESCENT
TABLE-WARE, WATER SETS, Etc.

Shades, Molasses Cans, Salts, Sugar Shakers, Oil Bottles,
etc , decorated in hand and printed patterns on bright or bisque
grounds.

The BUCKEYE GLASS CO.,

Martin's Ferry, Ohio.

January, 1889, advertisement from the Buckeye Glass Co. shows our strongest proof that the pattern formerly called BUBBLE LATTICE can now be renamed BUCKEYE LATTICE. The shape of the salt shaker on the left matches that of the shaker in this pattern (Fig. 372). The shaker on the right seems to match those in the "breakfast caster" shown on page 35

(office manager) at Buckeye. Under the same heading it stated, "Mr. Harry Northwood, manager of the Northwood, will have charge of the office for a while." I believe this to mean that he was taking over the secretarial vacancy left at Northwood's office by Mr. Kerr, and certainly not the offices of the Buckeye.

The patterns most definitely made by the Buckeye are REVERSE SWIRL, BIG WINDOWS (both made from the same shape molds) and BUCKEYE LATTICE (formerly BUBBLE LATTICE). A decorated salt shaker made in the latter pattern's shape mold is pictured in the ad shown above. This firm also made hall cylinder lamps in COIN-SPOT, and probably other standard designs like SWIRL and STRIPE.

No opalescent glass made by Buckeye is mentioned in trade journals after 1890, with the departure of John F. Miller. His influence on the production of blown opalescent is notable. We know sewing lamps were made in opalescent glass at his American Glass Co., in Anderson, Ind. (see history), as well as syrup pitchers and salt shakers. An AMERICAN tableware pattern was mentioned in trade journals of this year, but its nature is unknown. There is a strong possibility that CHRYSANTHEMUM SWIRL was one of the new lines made by this short-lived concern. Mr. Miller later introduced another look-alike to the REVERSE SWIRL, known today as COLLARED REVERSE SWIRL, when he managed the Model Flint Glass Works after 1893, but it was not made in cranberry. Only blue, white and yellow are known in this variant.

The Buckeye struggled on after 1890, returning to pressed tableware, opaque wares in pink and black [WINDER-MERE'S FAN, ACORN] and a heavy production in oil lamps, but were undermined by labor troubles, a number of factory fires (reportedly arson), and closed after a disastrous final fire which destroyed the factory in February, 1896. No Buckeye shaped patterns have ever been reproduced, so the molds were probably destroyed.

IMPORTANT JOURNAL QUOTES:
6/23/1887 P&GR
At the BUCKEYE GLASS WORKS business is still good, with encouraging prospects for the future. The season has been a very prosperous one and the management is well pleased over it. Only one furnace, the large 15-pot one, has been in use but this has always worked to perfection and has turned out a large amount of ware, very little of which will be left unsold when the bars are drawn. There are now many fine fancy goods in the sample rooms than ever and a visit to it will pay any person. A line of goods is ready for the fall trade which ought to meet with a quick sale. The number of the new plain and opalescent dew drop table set is 527 [BIG WINDOWS?], and it is a pretty thing. The decorated vase lamps, six patterns with decorated shades to match, are very handsome. In Venetian thread ware [OPALESCENT SWIRL?], plain and decorated, they have a water set, new shapes in oil and vinegar bottles, new shapes in molasses jugs and lamp chimneys, salts, lamps in blue, white and canary, and other articles. These Venetian goods are something the Buckeye has not been making and are very neat and the decorations show to good advantage on them. . . .

11/10/1887 P&GR (MARTIN'S FERRY.)
At the BUCKEYE GLASS WORKS immense quanitites of lamps of all kinds, fourteen inch dome ruby shades and other shades, opalescent cans, jugs, paste mold opalescent pitchers, finger bowls, ruby tumblers, Venetian rib chimneys, punch tumblers, novelties and other kinds of ware are being turned out which is shipped about as fast as manufactured. A new lamp with a blue bowl and flint foot is selling well, the new tank furnace running altogether on them. A new glory hole has been built for shades. It has been a long time since business was as good at the Buckeye as it is now.

1/5/1888 P&GR
*The new opalescent set of the BUCKEYE GLASS CO. is a daisy [a Victorian term meaning a beauty—not a flower]. It is just out and ready for the spring trade and all the dealers who have seen it have ordered freely. **The number is 528 and there are four colors of it, canary, blue, crystal and ruby** [REVERSE SWIRL]. In the same goods casters [in metal holders] and water sets will be made. The Buckeye is getting there in good shape. It shut down on Saturday for a week or ten days to take stock and make needed repairs. Several additions are being made. The middle furnace will probably be started in the near future. Business is good.*

NORTHWOOD GLASS COMPANY,
Martin's Ferry, Ohio (1888-1892)
THE NORTHWOOD GLASS COMPANY,
Ellwood City, Pa. (1892-1896)
THE NORTHWOOD COMPANY,
Indiana, Pa. (1896-late 1899)
NATIONAL GLASS COMPANY,
Operating NORTHWOOD GLASS WORKS (1900-04)
H. NORTHWOOD & COMPANY,
Wheeling, W. Va. (1902-1905)
H. NORTHWOOD COMPANY,
Wheeling, W. Va. (1905-24)

The confusion over the ownership and management of the various factories carrying the Northwood name will take much more space than this book allows. The finite details of the five factories using Mr. Northwood's name will have to await the publication of the two books, NORTH-WOOD GLASS—THE EARLY YEARS (1882-1902) and NORTHWOOD GLASS—THE LATER YEARS (1902-1924).

Briefly, however, the plants at the first two locations were one management team, and the last three were owned by three other companies in which Harry Northwood had part ownership or stock. He never owned his factories outright, and in fact during much of his career he was facing financial difficulty. In 1896 he had trouble paying a rent of $50 per month owed by his cousin, Charles O. Northwood, a glass engraver who did work for his company. In Harry Northwood's obituary, the first two concerns were described as business failures, despite the incredible beauty of the art glass and colored blown products being produced. Much of Northwood's blown opalescent came from these two factories.

The first company at Martin's Ferry was established in late 1887 at an abandoned Union Glass Company factory, by wealthy coal magnate Henry Helling (formerly of Buckeye, La Belle and Union) and others. He hired Harry Northwood to manage the new concern, naming the company after the famous glassmaker. Blown patterns like ROYAL IVY, ROYAL OAK, LEAF MOLD, AURORA (Prima Donna), JEWEL (Threaded Swirl), and others were some of the lines made here. The first mention of opalescent was in July, 1889, with "straw jars" in "P.O., F.O. and B.O." (CHRYSANTHEMUM SWIRL?). A February, 1890, note describes a No. 272 line in "salads, oils and salt and peppers" (pattern unknown). In January, 1891, three water and lemonade (tankard shape) sets were reviewed. However, a pattern matchup on these remains elusive.

In early 1892 the management saw fit to relocate the equipment and some workers to Ellwood City, Pa, where they began operations in October. The name of the company was changed slightly. Advertisements mentioned lines in Opalescent, Coraline, Onyx and Ruby (cranberry). In 1895, The No. 91 line was mentioned in flint, blue and pink opalescent, possibly DAISY AND FERN. In August, a No. 205 design was made in pint and quart jugs (pitchers). In January, 1896, the No. 217 POLKA DOT in the FANCY FANS shape mold was clearly described. This last design is extremely rare today, perhaps because the factory closed shortly after then, Mr. Northwood resigning and moving to Indiana, Pa. to reopen an abandoned factory there.

The Northwood Company was established independent of the former associates, partly financed by Mr. Northwood's uncle, Thomas E.A. Dugan (not to be confused with Thomas Dugan, Northwood's cousin). In March, 1896, opalescent

lemonade sets were advertised. Mr. Northwood was probably continuing production, in different shape molds, of the DAISY AND FERN and POLKA DOT patterns. The CHRISTMAS SNOWFLAKE water sets were also probably among these sets. A letterhead from this period includes a vase with this design. In 1898, Thomas Dugan and Clara Northwood (Harry's wife) purchased the plant and land which they leased prior to this. This unusual sale was probably because Harry was being sued by his former employers at Ellwood City for what they considered his abandonment of their operation, which failed shortly after he left.

In January, 1899, the OPALINE BROCADE (SPANISH LACE) pattern was introduced. This proved to be a major success, and remains popular with today's collectors. But in September of that year, Mr. Northwood and Mr. Dugan sold their interests in the factory to the National Glass Co. for $1.00 and other valuable considerations (probably stock). In December, 1899, Harry sailed to England with his family to represent the new National at their London sales office.

The Indiana, Pa. factory, which was called The Northwood Glass Works while under National's ownership, continued with production of blown opalescent. A January, 1900, journal describes a line in pink, canary, green and blue, probably a continuation of SPANISH LACE. DAISY AND FERN was also made at this time, but as far as I know it was never made originally in yellow opalescent. In 1903 the BLOWN TWIST and BLOWN DRAPERY water sets were being offered by Butler Bros., indicating a National/Northwood production period. The syrups in the "Indiana" ball-shaped mold and the sugar shakers and syrups in the "Nine Panel" mold were also made here around 1900-1904. The standard designs, COINSPOT, SWIRL, and STRIPE were also made at Indiana, Pa.

For the continuing history of the Indiana, Pa. factory, see the Dugan Glass Company, which took over in January, 1904.

In late 1902 through 1903 there were two different factories carrying the name Northwood. The second and final Northwood company was established at the long-abandoned Hobbs' Wheeling factory in 1902. Mr. Northwood sold his interests in the National in 1901, and after losing an election to the presidency of this conglomerate, approached the Wheeling Board of Trade with a proposal to refurbish and reopen the plant in their city. Again with the help of his uncle T.E.A. Dugan, and financial incentives from the board, this was accomplished. By November of 1902, the new lines being made here included at least one opalescent blown design, probably Opalescent POINSETTIA. A trade journal describes a water set with "flowers and foliage which seem to stick right out" in colors of flint, blue, canary and pink. Shards of this pattern have been unearthed at the Wheeling factory site. These were previously thought to have been a Hobbs, Brockunier product, reissued by Northwood. I now feel they are exclusive to Northwood.

Blown opalescent was no longer popular enough after 1905 to warrant extensive production. Perhaps it was too fragile for the hard use required, and the costs did not warrant its continued production. Certainly the cranberry color was no longer popular at the end of the Victorian era. The industry was rethinking its future when the National folded. There was a shift to cheaper "tank glass", imitation-cut pressed designs and, in 1907, the popular iridescent tableware known today as "carnival glass".

The Northwood Wheeling factory remained successful until Harry's death in 1919, when he died of dropsy. The company entered bankruptcy in 1925, never to be reopened.

See the Northwood section for trade journal quotes describing his glass, history and life and further information on this glass genius.

1899 Pitkins and Brooks catalogue pictures this assortment of SPANISH LACE which the catalogue called BROCADE. The original factory name for this line was OPALINE BROCADE. The shape molds used on the set are the same ones used on the UTOPIA OPTIC pattern. Note the original stopper in the cruet, which appears to be a pressed faceted stopper

1897 Pitkins and Brooks wholesale catalogue pictures three opalescent water sets (with six tumblers) in COINSPOT, SWIRL and DAISY AND FERN patterns. All three were made by The Northwood Company, Indiana. Pa. The water sets at the bottom of this page are described as Austrian

Another page from same 1899 Pitkins and Brooks catalogue shows a DAISY AND FERN cruet with a cut stopper. Note this cruet is listed as No. 191. The Northwood chart on page 11 includes a No. 91 set described in an 1895 trade journal, but this appears to be a misprint by the reporter. DAISY AND FERN was probably introduced at Northwood's Ellwood City, Pa., factory, but some of the molds were moved to the new Indiana, Pa., location in 1896

23

AMERICAN GLASS COMPANY
Anderson, Indiana
(mid-1889—late 1890)

This new factory was opened by the former management of the Buckeye Glass Co., John F. Miller and Andrew Gottschalk, and advertised a line of tableware in "fancy colors", opalescent and "marblescent" lamps, and a large variety of items, all in the style made earlier by Buckeye. Mr. Miller held a patent No. 393,257 (filed on 11/20/1888) for "opalescent glass with ridges and spiral stripes" (probably REVERSE SWIRL), and may have produced a line of similar nature at his own Anderson factory. Molds were made for the new company at Martin's Ferry, probably by Hipkins Novelty Mold Co.

The one table line most probably made by American is CHRYSANTHEMUM SWIRL. A July, 1890 ad described lamps with iron or brass feet, in which this pattern is known (*Thuro1, p. 235*).

The life of the company was short-lived, just over a year. It began operations in June, 1889. In early 1890, Mr. Gottschalk returned to Buckeye. The Anderson factory closed shortly after the appearance of an advertisement in June, 1890, which included no illustrations. In early 1891, the factory was sold and became the Hoosier Glass Co., a manufacturer of prescription ware. Mr. Miller went to work for Eagle Glass Co., then was located at Riverside Glass, and by 1901 was manager of the Model Flint Glass Co., at Albany, Ind., where blown opalescent (including a "collared" version of REVERSE SWIRL) was again produced.

If American made CHRYSANTHEMUM SWIRL, it also made the rare OPALESCENT COBWEB pattern lamp (*Thuro2, p. 101-l*) which was from the same shape mold.

It is possible that the Fig. 60 water pitcher was made by American Glass Co. It is similar to REVERSE SWIRL and CHRYSANTHEMUM SWIRL in nature. However, there is no evidence to support such an attribution. It is NOT the "Collared" variant of REVERSE SWIRL made later by Miller at Albany. That rare pitcher is shown in *Bond, p. 13*, and was probably never made in cranberry.

IMPORTANT TRADE QUOTE:
6/13/1889 C&GJ

ANDERSON, IND.—A visit to the new American Glass Works here will convince anyone that it is a model for completeness and convenience. The works are now in operation, and they will spend this month in getting out samples of lamps of all varieties and novelties in fancy colors and decorations, and fancy toilet articles, water sets, etc. Novelties will be the specialty of the American, and the outlook for them is very ... Messrs. John F. Miller and A. Gottschalk are the active members of the company in charge, and their well-matured ideas will no doubt bring them a good trade right from the start. They are to be congratulated on the completeness of their plant.

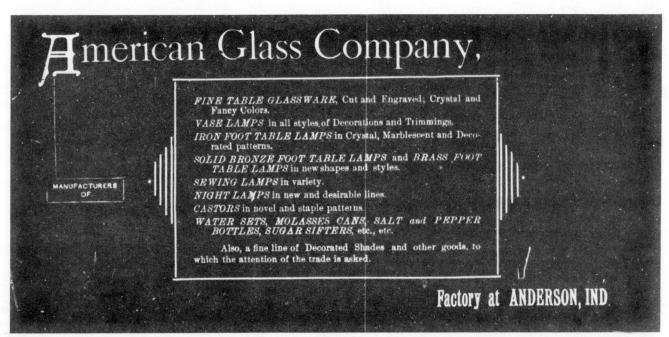

July, 1890 Crockery & Glass Journal *advertisement of the American Glass Co., Anderson, Ind., which was started by John F. Miller, well versed in the production of blown opalescent. Note that the ad mentions water sets, molasses cans, sugar sifters, salt and pepper bottles, night lamps, and table glassware in "fancy colors". This ad is our strongest evidence that American Glass made CHRYSANTHEMUM SWIRL. Note the listing of solid bronze and brass footed table lamps. A lamp with such a foot is known in this pattern (or a similar copy). The factory was closed a few months after the appearance of this advertisement*

NICKEL-PLATE GLASS COMPANY
Fostoria, Ohio
(1888-1893)

This factory's contribution to blown opalescent is based on years of previous experience by the management in the field. The president of the concern, established in 1888, was A. J. Smith, formerly with La Belle, the secretary-treasurer and head salesman was B.M. Hildreth, formerly with Hobbs, and the factory manager was J.B. Russell, also formerly with Hobbs. However, the Opalescent SWIRL and WIDE STRIPE designs as well as some shapes in DOUBLE GREEK KEY, seem to have been the limited output in blown opalescent. The colors known are white, blue, canary and cranberry opalescent. The company joined the U.S. Glass Co. in 1891 and the factory was closed in 1893.

IMPORTANT JOURNAL QUOTE:
1/14/1891 CG&L

*The Nickel Plate Glass Co., of Fostoria, Ohio, have their interests attended to by Mr. W. A. Rolf in Room 152. They show a large assortment of goods. The new pattern, No. 77, "Royal" ware is a handsome one and they have a full line of it, comprising salvers and bowls, footed or without feet, casseroles, high-footed bowls with covers, oval dishes or candy trays, low-footed comports and several other articles. These are all fire polished and highly finished. The line contains over 40 pieces, and they make it engraved as well as plain. The handles on the various articles are very pretty and conveniently placed. The company also manufacture **a line of blown and pressed opalescent ware, among which are pitchers of several sizes, molasses cans, sugar sifters, salts, peppers, oil bottles, water bottles, finger bowls, etc.;** also staples, such as tumblers, goblets, ales, beer mugs, berry sets, lamps, etc. . . .*

Assortment of lamps from a circa 1892 U.S. Glass (Factory N) catalogue.

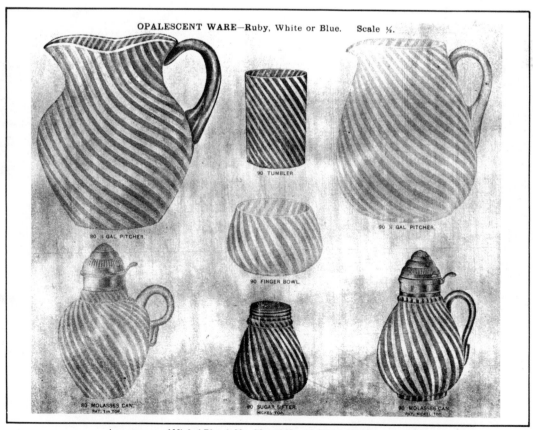

Assortment of Nickel Plate's No. 80 and No. 90 OPAL SWIRL, which was continued by U.S. Glass after 1891

25

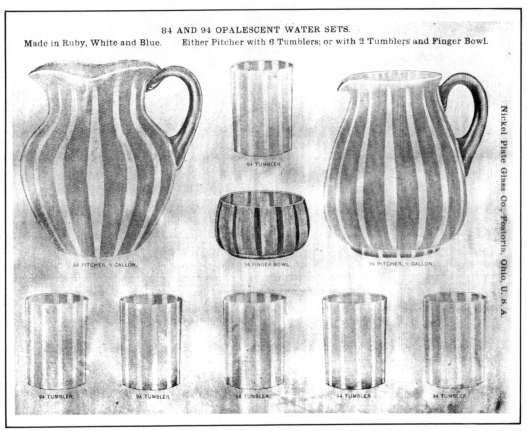

Assortment of Nickel Plate's No. 84 and No. 94 WIDE STRIPE pitchers, tumblers and finger bowls, from circa 1891 U. S. Glass catalogue. The shape of the pitcher on the right is very similar to one later used by Imperial Glass Company in the 1930's (see page 65)

FOSTORIA SHADE & LAMP CO.
Fostoria, Ohio (1890-1894)

CONSOLIDATED LAMP & GLASS CO.
Fostoria, Ohio (1894-1896)

Originally known as the Fostoria Shade and Lamp Co., this firm was established with the participation of Nicholas Kopp and Charles Etz, who left Hobbs Glass Co. in 1890. It was a new factory, built partly by the former Governor of Ohio, Charles Foster. In 1893, the firm released a No. 93 line of tableware, which they referred to as "Cable", which may be the pattern we now call Consolidated's CRISS CROSS. In 1894, the name of the firm was changed after merging with the jobbing firm Wallace & McAfee Co., with headquarters at Pittsburgh. A new factory was built at Coraopolis, Pa., and after a fire at Fostoria in 1896, the workers were moved to the Pennsylvania factory. The firm specialized in Kopp cased colors, producing some of the most beautiful lamps and shades, as well as some tableware. Lamps and lighting ware remained a specialty until the late 1920's, when the firm began production of their MARTELE' line of tableware and vases. Due to depressed economic conditions, in 1933 the factory shut down for a few years, selling glass from remaining stock, and reopened in 1936 as a new organization. The factory closed finally and forever in 1964.

THE ELSON GLASS COMPANY (1882-1893)
WEST VIRGINIA GLASS COMPANY (1893-1896)
WEST VIRGINIA GLASS MFG. COMPANY (1897-late 1899)
NATIONAL GLASS CO.—Operating WEST VIRGINIA GLASS WORKS (1899-1903) Martin's Ferry, Ohio

There were at least five different companies operating this Martin's Ferry factory. The Elson firm failed during the depression of 1893.

The only blown opalescent made by the original Elson firm seems to be a caster set, made from molds acquired from Belmont Glass Co. One of the original directors was Charles Muhleman, who later ran this firm after a reorganization in 1896.

The blown opalescent made by West Virginia Glass Co. during its two years in business can be easily understood when we pinpoint the organizers, who took over and reorganized the old Elson Glass Co. After being idle for six months, in late 1893 the factory was remodeled and restarted by Hanson E. Waddell, with Percy Beaumont as mold designer and chemist. The new company started up after U.S. Glass closed the old Hobbs factory, which Waddell managed, across the river at Wheeling, and the first lines made include lines in blown opalescent. These include their POLKA DOT and FERN in the No. 203 OPTIC molds.

The firm made blown opalescent and pressed glass until mid-1895, when hard times hit the new organization and the factory shut down for almost a year. Mr. Waddell became a salesman for McKee and later Heisey. Percy Beaumont left to open his own decorating firm (see history) at the abandoned Northwood factory in the same town.

The factory was sold in early 1896 to some of the bondholders of the plant and reorganized with a slight name change and a different directorate which included former secretaries Ed Muhleman and Andrew J. Smith. But glass was not made until March of 1897. There appears to have been a merger, perhaps to raise capital, with the Specialty Glass Works of East Liverpool, Oh. Two owners of the closed factory at that location are listed as directors of West Virginia Glass Mfg. Co. in 1898.

In late 1899, the factory joined National Glass, and in 1901 the factory was operated by Crystal Glass Co. at nearby Bridgeport, as a second branch plant, both independent of the parent company. The West Virginia factory closed in 1903, after the resignation of Muhleman in 1901, who was building his Imperial factory in Bellaire.

IMPORTANT JOURNAL QUOTES:
1/14/1893 CG&L
ELSON GLASS CO., MARTIN'S FERRY, O.—This concern has a neat display in Room 16. The company make

both lime and lead glass and have a large assortment of both. They have a new pattern called the "Gem", plain, engraved, etched and cut, and it will hold its place with anything in the market. They have a beautiful line of ruby-stained glass and don't take a back seat from anyone in this specialty. The "De Soto" is another fine line they offer, engraved and etched, and it is a decidedly handsome one. This is headquarters for **casters**, *of which they have a great many sizes and styles. They make a nice line of* **opalescent ware** *too. Pressed bar goods, tumblers, stemware, water bottles and a number of other miscellaneous articles are among the assortment.*

JOURNAL QUOTE:
12/20/1893 CG&L
MARTIN'S FERRY, O.—The West Virginia Glass Co. have three complete lines of new goods and a lot of new specialties, all of which promise to be fast sellers. In the "Gem" ware there are four different effects, consisting of crystal, engraved, etched and cut No. 4, all finely finished. No. 203 is a pressed line, imitation of blown and there will be at least two decorations in this. It looks very much like blown. Another of the new lines is No. 204. This is blown and will be made in fancy colors, and there is quite a variety of it. The two new lines of novelties consist of sweetmeats, celeries, olives, etc. All of the above goods are entirely new and will be ready for the spring trade. . . .

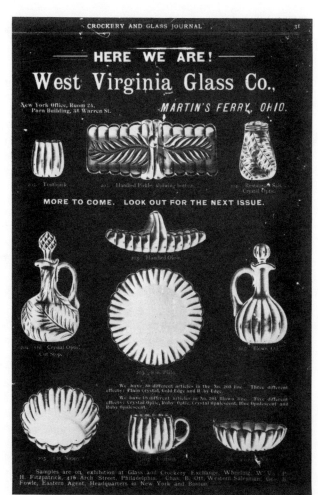

January, 1894 advertisement picturing two items in West Virginia Glass Co.'s No. 204 OPALESCENT FERN pattern. Note the original cut stopper in the cruet. Some pieces of FERN were blown into the No. 203 WEST VIRGINIA OPTIC shape molds

Another January, 1894 advertisement from West Virginia Glass Co. The sugar shaker pictured is from the shape mold used for the OPALESCENT FERN pattern

LEMONADE SET, BY THE WEST VIRGINIA GLASS MFG. CO.

A January, 1899 Crockery & Glass Journal *pictured this lemonade set in POLKA DOT by West Virginia Glass Mfg. Co., Martin's Ferry, Oh. Note the unusual clover-leaf top on the pitcher. It is uncertain if this pattern was made at the same time (1894) as the FERN pattern, but both shared common shape molds. POLKA DOT can also be found in plain, non-opalescent colors. The design was copied by Northwood at Ellwood City and Indiana, Pa., and his original spot molds were used on a line of reproductions by L.G. Wright*

Close-up of paper label found on base of COLLARED REVERSE SWIRl covered butter (see page 72). The reference to this as the Model Fli Glass WORKS proves it was made after the National Glass Co. merg in late 1899. This variant of the REVERSE SWIRL motif was one several designs made by John F. Miller, who was managing the Moc Flint plant in 1902, just prior to their closing late that year

MODEL FLINT GLASS CO.
Albany, Ind.
(Late 1893-1899)

NATIONAL GLASS CO.
Operating Model Flint Glass Works
(1900-1902)

This company originally began production at Findlay, Ohio, but was induced to move the works to Albany, Ind. in late 1893. At first the firm made only pressed tableware in clear glass. The factory was absorbed into the National Glass Co. in late 1899. With the acquisition of John F. Miller as manager in 1901, who earlier introduced designs in blown opalescent at Buckeye and his own American Glass Co. at nearby Anderson, Ind., a variety of blown items were introduced by Model Flint. But the blown "fancy glass" made here was limited, as the factory was closed by National some time in late 1902. An October, 1902 trade journal gave this optimistic viewpoint from Mr. Miller:

John F. Miller, manager of the National's plant at Albany, Ind., and formerly with the Buckeye at Martin's Ferry and the Riverside at Wellsburg, was in Wheeling a few days ago and reports the glass business is brisk and all factories in his company working to the limit.

This factory made opalescent pressed ware in patterns like WREATH AND SHELL (OMN: MANILA) and RIBBED SPIRAL, and a variety of novelties. But some blown opalescent was also made here, all in the earlier style used by Miller at Buckeye and American. The "Collared" variant of REVERSE SWIRL was definitely made here, as a covered butter with the original factory sample label is known. It also appears that the popular motifs in STRIPE, SWIRL and FERN were made here, based on shards found at the factory site. However, some of the items shown in Bond, p. 17 *are from shape molds used at other factories, and are not Model Flint products.*

There is a probability that no cranberry opalescent was made at this factory. COLLARED REVERSE SWIRL is not known in this color, and neither is the unusual OPALESCENT FERN pitcher shown on the cover of Bond. Nor are any of the other blown shapes pictured in Bond which seem to be known Albany glass shapes and colors.

IMPORTANT JOURNAL QUOTE:
9/12/1901 C&GJ

A number of new designs, decorations, etc. are being shown this fall from the different factories of the National. The Model flint works are making a line of opalescent specialties and novelties in yellow and blue that are dainty and unique. They comprise card baskets and cases, vases, rose bowls, pond lily sherbets, chrysanthemum holders, etc [all pressed glass]. A solid opal stein, an excellent imitation of pottery, is a notable new creation. The Model also shows two new lines of crystal tableware.

1/2/1902 C&GJ

The Model Flint Glass Works sends a large variety of decorated opalescent novelties in canary and blue. They are dainty and attractive.

BEAUMONT GLASS COMPANY
 Martin's Ferry, O. (1895-1902)
 Grafton, W. Va. (1902-1906)

It is unknown when Percy Beaumont, brother of Harry Northwood's wife Clara, first came to America. He was working for his brother-in-law in 1889 at The Northwood Glass Company, at Martin's Ferry, but probably worked at either La Belle or Hobbs, Brockunier prior to this year. In 1890, he resigned his position as shipping clerk at Northwood's factory to accept a position for Hobbs as a "metal maker and decorator." Here he remained until July 1893. Later the Hobbs factory was closed by the new owners, the U. S. Glass Company, in October, 1893. Mr. Beaumont, along with Hobbs' manager Hanson E. Waddell and other workers from the Wheeling factory, moved across the river to a new concern being organized at the old Elson Glass Company factory at Martin's Ferry, O. This firm was renamed the West Virginia Glass Co. Here he was described as a "metal maker and chemist."

No doubt, Mr. Beaumont helped design the two major opalescent lines made by this firm, POLKA DOT and FERN. But in late 1895, he and other gentlemen established a decorating concern at the abandoned Northwood factory in the same town (Harry's firm had relocated to Ellwood City, Pa.). For three years this new Beaumont Glass Co. built a healthy business decorating the glass made by other factories, including patterns by Riverside and McKee & Bros. However, in 1899, after briefly considering relocating to Northwood's abandoned Ellwood City factory (Harry had moved by then to Indiana, Pa.), the Martin's Ferry plant was refurbished for the actual manufacture of glass and a number of opalescent blown patterns and pressed glass lines were introduced. Some of the patterns were copies (or reissues from the original molds) of lines possibly designed earlier by Beaumont at Hobbs, particularly SEAWEED, STARS & STRIPES, WINDOWS and SWIRL. He also produced a copy of one of his West Virginia designs, FERN. His No. 27 "Bitter Bottle" (H3, p. 61) is a shape which has been copied by L.G. Wright for their line of reproductions. The ever-popular COINSPOT was also made in a water set. A new design, DAISY IN CRISS-CROSS, was also made.

No opalescent glass is mentioned in trade journals after 1901, as the firm concentrated on decorated pressed tableware and blown lemonade sets. Mr. Beaumont resigned as president in 1901, but remained on with the firm, which relocated in 1902 to a new factory in Grafton, W. Va. The old Northwood factory was re-opened as the Haskins Glass Co., a manufacturer of electrical lighting goods. Haskins then moved into the abandoned West Virginia Glass factory in 1906. The old Northwood/Beaumont factory burned down in 1909, never to be rebuilt.

It appears no blown opalescent was made at the Grafton factory. Mr. Beaumont sold his interests in the firm in 1906 and the name of the factory was changed to the Tygert Valley Glass Co. Beaumont later became manager of the Union Stopper Co. at Morgantown, a manufacturer of stationer's goods, and when this firm closed he established another factory, possibly a decorating firm, later a lighting ware factory, which operated long past Mr. Beaumont's death in 1948.

The best documentation of Beaumont's contributions to blown opalescent can be found in the circa 1900 catalogue reprint in K7, pls. 58-68. These pages are reprinted in this book courtesy Kamm Publications.

IMPORTANT JOURNAL QUOTES:
8/31/1899 C&GJ

The Beaumont Glass Co. have got their glassmaking department in full operation and are now turning out all their own ware for decoration. Their line of opalescent is very attractive and cannot fail to meet with a liberal demand by reason of its beauty and intrinsic merit. Their shades and tints and shapes attract at sight. Mr. Beaumont is an expert color and glass man and his skill is represented in all their work. No. 99, "Admiral" set [FLORA pattern], is opalescent, gold-footed—in shades from brown to pearl. It has a gold edge and tasty gold decors. It is quaint, rich and elegant. They have a great variety of lemonade sets that are opalescent. The patterns are all pretty. No. 24 is a reversed dot [WINDOWS]; No. 11 a large dot [COINSPOT]; 16 a spiral twist [SWIRL]. They are putting out this week a new set in ruby, crystal and blue opalescent, with fern body [OPALESCENT FERN]. It is dainty and will win admiration.

9/7/1899 C&GJ

Alex P. Menzies, the New York representative of the Beaumont Glass Co., has full lines of that company's ware and is showing their latest creation for the first time this week.

It is a line of jugs in opalescent white, red and blue, with a field of stars at the bottom and stripes running up the jug.

The shapes are excellent. He has also just opened a line of crystal, sapphire and canary opalescent with gold decorations that are new and pretty.

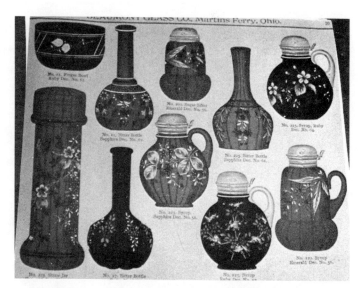

This Beaumont Glass Co. circa 1899 catalogue page is reprinted in original color in H3. The shape mold used on the No. 225 straw jar may be the same one used to shape the Fig. 246 OPAL SWIRL straw jar, and matches one (which had a finial) made earlier by Hobbs Glass Co. The No. 27 "Bitter Bottle" is the melon-rib shape copied by L.G. Wright. The ball-shaped syrups, shown here with and without collared bases, could easily be confused for a similar shape found on the "Indiana" Ball-shape syrup. The ACORN syrup and sugar shaker were made earlier in opaque colors by Buckeye Glass Co., which burned down several years before. Thus, Beaumont either bought old molds from factories no longer operating, or copied some of his shapes from previously existing designs

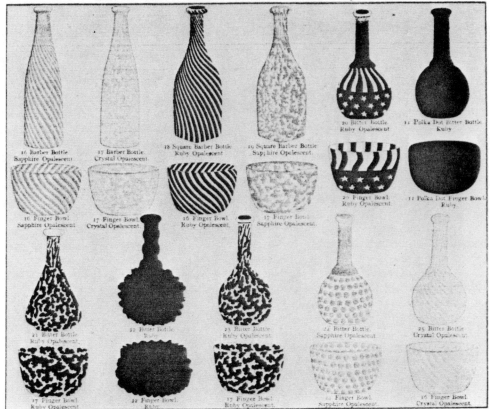

From Beaumont Glass Co. catalogue, circa 1899. Except for the placement of the OPAL STARS AND STRIPES bitter bottle and finger bowl, and the assignment of new numbers, this page is virtually identical to that found in a circa 1891 U.S. Glass Co., Factory H (formerly Hobbs), catalogue page reprinted on page 17. It is possible that Percy Beaumont designed some of these patterns for Hobbs before he moved to West Virginia Glass Co. in 1893. He undoubtedly acquired the molds for these items from U.S. Glass in 1899, when Mr. Beaumont began manufacturing glass at Martin's Ferry, Oh., factory (the same one used earlier by his brother-in-law, Harry Northwood)

BEAUMONT GLASS CO., Martins Ferry, Ohio.

This page includes an oil cruet in OPALESCENT SEAWEED and a syrup in DAISY IN CRISS CROSS

Three lemonade sets in OPALESCENT STARS & STRIPES, WINDOWS and FERN patterns. The first two were probably made from old Hobbs U.S. Glass molds. The latter is a copy of a pattern Beaumont introduced while associated with the West Virginia Glass Co.

Assortment of lemonade and water sets in OPALESCENT SEAWEED, SWIRL and COINSPOT patterns. All three patterns were produced earlier by Hobbs, and it is virtually impossible to differentiate the Hobbs from the Beaumont

DUGAN GLASS COMPANY
Indiana, Pa.
(1904-1913)

According to INDIANA COUNTY PENNSYLVANIA—HER PEOPLE PAST AND PRESENT (1913), Thomas E. Dugan arrived in America in 1881, and like his more famous cousin Harry Northwood, began his career in America at Hobbs, Brockunier & Co., Buckeye, Northwood (Ellwood City) and as manager of the Indiana, Pa. factory for National Glass (formerly The Northwood Company). He was related to Thomas E. A. Dugan, a wealthy capitalist from Ellwood City, Pa. who is known to have financed Harry Northwood's independent ventures at Indiana, Pa., and Wheeling, W. Va. For years, Thomas Dugan remained in the shadows of his cousin and uncle. But in 1904, he had finally come into his own, when he, along with others, organized the Dugan Glass Co., purchasing the Indiana, Pa., factory from the disbanding National combine for $22,500.

Whereas blown opalescent was being made by this firm during its earliest years as an independent (1904-1913), by 1910 the firm was deeply involved in the production of iridescent pressed glass known today as "carnival glass". This company is known to have produced the popular COINSPOT, SWIRL and DAISY & FERN patterns, at least in the NINE-PANEL and WIDE WAIST sugar shaker molds. Water sets were also made in all three patterns. Syrup pitchers and cruets were also made here in their own particular shape molds. Perhaps the most unique pattern made by Dugan was the SWASTIKA, a tankard water pitcher in blue opalescent known in their DIAMONDS AND CLUBS shape mold. No doubt, other patterns were made here, as some of the molds introduced during the earlier Northwood and National regimes remained at the factory site (some acquired by L.G. Wright in the late 1930's). Perhaps Dugan continued some production of the SPANISH LACE pattern, introduced by Northwood in 1899 as OPALINE BROCADE.

In 1913, Thomas Dugan resigned from the firm and the company was renamed the Diamond Glass-Ware Co., by which it was known until the plant burned down in 1931. After 1913, Mr. Dugan had brief associations with a number of other concerns, Cambridge, Mound Valley and a new Dugan Glass Co. (at Lonaconing) before settling in relative anonymity with Anchor Hocking at Lancaster.

IMPORTANT JOURNAL QUOTE:
1/16/1904 CG&L

If I have as much pleasure in writing of as I had in seeing the stock of the new Dugan Glass Co., which was until last week the old Northwood Glass Works, Indiana, Pa., and now represented by W.G. Minnemeyer, I shall be greatly pleased. And if I am at all able to decipher my notes I expect to have quite as much. To begin:

The first thing that flashed upon my vision was a crystal **opalescent epergne** *in which a number of nice black cigars gracefully reposed. Then the next, were some green square candlesticks which one could imagine being the admired centre of a ladies' luncheon table. A new line of tableware, which comes in everything from a punch bowl to a toothpick, is called the Nation [S-REPEAT]. The glass is pressed with designs of parallel scroll, I think Mr. Minnemeyer called it— and has a decoration of white and gold enamel. The entire line comes in green and amethyst and blue and crystal.*

The New York line [formerly Northwood's SHELL, now known to be Dugan] is pressed in a shell effect. This line is almost as big as its name, as it comes in opalescent and two plain colors undecorated and the three decorated in gold. This is a general line, too. Picture to yourself forty different styles of giddy lemonade sets in four colors. These range all the way from the very cheap to the ones heavily embossed in gold and ruby stain. One of these sets introduces a new shape in tumblers called Touraine. Yet this is not all. There are fifty "new novelties" in **opalescent dusters**, *which is a queer name, I think, for respectable sugar shakers. Then there is going to be an immense line of night lamps which no doubt will have arrived long before this. The ones I saw were most attractive particularly one which Mr. Minnemeyer likened to a Chinese pagoda. All success to the new management.*

The Indiana "Ball-shape" syrup is shown here from a 1908 Butler Bros. catalogue, indiciating that old Northwood molds from before the National Glass merger were still being used after the factory became the Dugan Glass Company

A 1903 Butler Bros. catalogue pictured a COINSPOT and DAISY AND FERN pitcher, made by National Glass Co. at their Northwood Glass Works (Indiana, Pa.) factory. These were offerred here in flint, blue and green opalescent, but both are also known in cranberry. The COINSPOT is also known in yellow opalescent

JEFFERSON GLASS COMPANY
Steubenville, Ohio (1900-1907)
Follansbee, WV (1907-1933)

This firm remodeled an abandoned factory in Steubenville, O., in September, 1900, and began making glass the following month. Many of the original organizers and factory management had experience producing opalescent glass. The first president was Harry Bastow, earlier with Northwood at Indiana, Pa. The sales manager was George Mortimer, also long associated with Northwood. The Fenton brothers were also a part of this new concern. The Jefferson opalescent blown patterns date from about 1901-1907, prior to their relocating to a brand new factory built by a reorganized firm in 1906. They began making glass at Follansbee, W. Va., in 1907. After 1907, there is no mention of opalescent in pressed or blown form being made by Jefferson. In 1908, the firm acquired the rights to the popular CHIPPENDALE pattern and the Krys-Tol trademark, along with the designer Benjamin Jacobs, who became one of the managers. But in 1910 the firm again was sold, to a former Macbeth-Evans manager, Harry Schnellbaugh, and his partners, who eventually transformed the tableware factory into a lighting ware manufacturer. The firm went bankrupt in 1933.

The best documentation of Jefferson blown opalescent is a catalogue page reprinted in *K7, pl. 43*, clearly from the earlier Steubenville location. The catalogue from which this was taken, which I have studied at Oglebay Institute Mansion Museum (Wheeling), shows water sets and crimped salad bowls in patterns like COINSPOT, SWIRL, BUTTONS AND BRAIDS and SWIRLING MAZE. Frank Fenton later copied the shape and patterns of some of these water sets when he opened his own factory at Williamstown.

IMPORTANT TRADE QUOTE:
1/10/1901 CG&L

*JEFFERSON GLASS CO. — George Mortimer occupies room 102 here with a most gorgeous line of samples of the Jefferson Glass Co., Steubenville, O. A page or two might be easily written on this display without by any means exhausting the subject, but there is no necessity for it as all interested in glass will be anxious to see it. The company's specialty is colored and decorated ware but they have some fine crystal as well. **They have a number of elegant lemonade sets in green, blue, ruby, crystal and opalescent with ornate effects in gold and enamel. These in many new shapes not shown before . . .***

Circa 1908 catalogue page from Jefferson Glass Co., showing lemonade sets in BUTTONS AND BRAIDS, OPAL SWIRL and COINSPOT. Jefferson discontinued the production of "fancy glass" shortly after this catalogue was printed, entering other specialized fields (pressed Krys-Tol, lighting ware) after 1909

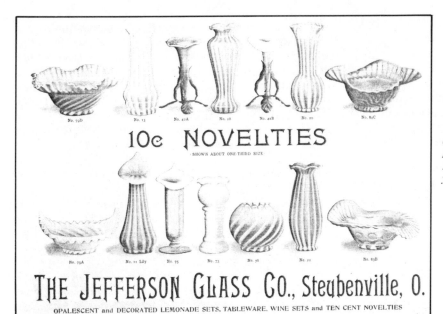

Circa 1902 assortment of ten cent novelties using OPAL-ESCENT SWIRL, STRIPE, COINSPOT and SWIRLING MAZE patterns. All of these are known in white, blue, yellow, green and cranberry opalescent colors

A Spring, 1904 Butler Bros. catalogue pictured a SWIRLING MAZE water pitcher in the same shape mold used for Jefferson's COINSPOT. This shape is different from the other two known shapes shown on page 92

A February, 1909, Butler Bros. pictured this assortment of BUTTONS AND BRAIDS, COINSPOT and SWIRL water sets—here called "serpentine, polka dot and scroll".

BASTOW GLASS COMPANY
Coudersport, Pa.
(10/1903—5/1904)

Mr. Harry Bastow started his active connection with the flint glass industry when he became associated with Harry Northwood at Ellwood City, Pa., in 1895, and succeeded Mr. Northwood in charge of the Northwood plant at Indiana, Pa., and when Mr. Northwood went to London for the National, he reportedly turned over his formulas to Mr. Bastow.

Mr. Bastow took up the study of chemistry, with special reference to glass, and developed a number of color and decorative effects, as well as patenting a number of mechanical improvements.

In 1900, he and others from the Indiana factory left the National and established a competing "fancy glass" factory in Steubenville, Oh. This was the Jefferson Glass Co., where cranberry opalescent was also made, and Mr. Bastow was the first President. Never very happy sharing the limelight, Mr. Bastow established his own glass company in a former tile factory at Coudersport, Pa. Following him here were future business partners, Frank and John Fenton. The Coudersport factory began making glass in October, 1903, showing their wares at the 1904 Pittsburgh exhibition. The glass made was very much like the former product made at Northwood and Jefferson, including blown opalescent, pressed glass in opalescent, opal and custard, and decorated lemonade sets. But their contribution to this field was limited, and probably no cranberry opalescent was ever made here, for the factory burned down only seven months later, on May 1, 1904, and was never rebuilt.

Later there was talk of his reopening the old Northwood factory at Ellwood City, Pa., and for a while he managed the Haskins Glass Co. There was another Bastow Glass Co., a manufacturer of lighting ware, at Weston, W. Va., around 1909. In 1912, Bastow was with the West Virginia Optical Glass Co., at Wheeling. Perhaps Harry Bastow's major contribution to glass history, and the art of blown opalescent glass production, was his association with the Fenton brothers in helping establish their factory in Williamstown, W. Va., which continues the production of blown opalescent glass today.

OTHER MANUFACTURERS OF BLOWN OPALESCENT

DALZELL, GILMORE & LEIGHTON CO., Findlay, Ohio
KING GLASS CO., Pittsburgh, Pa.
CENTRAL GLASS WORKS, Wheeling, W. Va.
BELMONT GLASS COMPANY, Bellaire, Ohio
MT. WASHINGTON GLASS WORKS, New Bedford, Mass.

There were other factories which I believe made blown opalescent pattern glass, but in such limited quanitities that they are not featured above. First and foremost, there is Dalzell, Gilmore & Leighton of Findlay, Ohio, manufacturers of the ROSE ONYX in 1889. The original name for this appears to be "Floradine". Except for perhaps Mt. Washington, it seems that no cranberry opalescent was made at King Glass Co., Pittsburgh, and Central Glass Co., Wheeling, both absorbed by U.S. Glass. It is possible that the opalescent fount lamps with King and Central bases were produced at other U.S. Glass locations (Hobbs or Nickel-Plate), as many molds were moved around after the 1891 merger. The Belmont Glass Works at Bellaire made a caster set in opalescent, and a syrup in COINSPOT, but since they sold some of their molds to Elson Glass Co. (which became West Virginia Glass Co.), perhaps the cranberry color in these patterns was made by the new owners. And finally, the Mt. Washington Glass Works may have produced some cranberry opalescent. A Pairpoint catalogues reprinted in *Padgett*, pp. 22 and 65, show what may be Mt. Washington opalescent. However, the same p. 22 shows a Hobbs FRANCES WARE SWIRL celery tray in a Pairpoint frame.

Undoubtedly, there will be other small or short-lived factories which made some of the extremely rare items found on today's collectors' market. Comparing the information in my Book 2, *Opalescent Glass From A to Z*, and this new Book 9 is a profound testament to the difference in knowledge 12 years can make. Computers, cooperation among fellow researchers, and my own growing interest in "history", and not just "glass", has made all this new information possible.

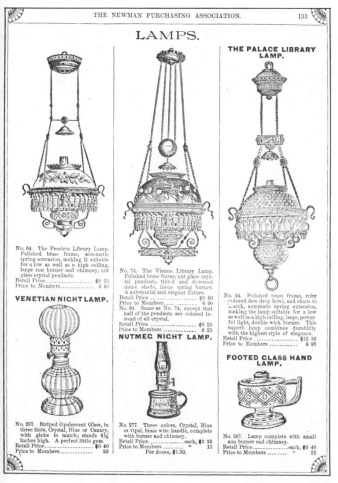

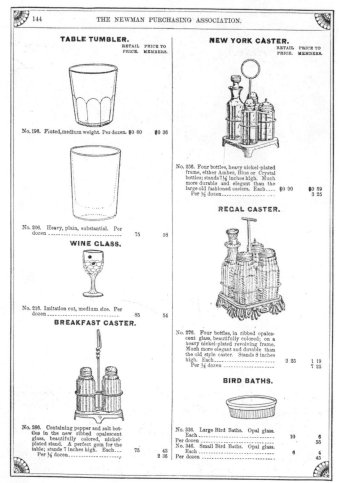

An 1888 Newman Purchasing Association (Chicago) wholesale catalogue illustrated caster sets and a night lamp in OPALESCENT STRIPE. The lamp and "breakfast caster" appear to be Buckeye (compare shape of shaker, p. 21, top right), but the "regal caster" set was made by Belmont Glass Co., Bridgeport, Oh. The molds for this caster set and others were later sold to ELSON GLASS CO. (which became West Virginia Glass).

IDENTIFICATION CLUES ON NORTHWOOD GLASS

There are certain molding characteristics that were used by Harry Northwood at his different companies that may help collectors in identifying Northwood patterns.

Partly based on patterns which we know were exclusively Northwood, SPANISH LACE, CHRISTMAS SNOWFLAKE, DAISY AND FERN (N. Swirl mold), etc., a pattern can be determined concerning his other lines. Northwood designed many of his cranberry opalescent patterns around molds used for other lines. For instance, the Northwood Swirl mold was used in creating the DAISY AND FERN. While there are many reproductions in this opalescent pattern, none of these swirled shapes have been reproduced.

The APPLE BLOSSOM shape mold was also used with the DAISY AND FERN motif (Fig. 26), as was also the QUILTED PHLOX and the RIBBED PILLAR molds combined with LATTICE (see Figs. 108, 110 and 241). His ROYAL IVY and JEWEL shape molds have been found with a SWIRL motif.

One feature that Northwood often used in shaping his patterns was the use of a particular base plate construction. The rim or "Marie" around the base of these pieces varies from ¼″ to ½″ depending on the size of this vessel. This marie serves as a flat resting area for the particular piece of glass. This base is shown here on the base of the Spanish Lace.

However, other firms may have used this type of base plate on their molds, but we are concerned here primarily with blown opalescent. Using this base as a "final" source of attribution is used only when combined with other corroborative evidence.

Another characteristic is the special handle sometimes found on Northwood pieces. I call this the "question mark" handle, as can be seen on Figs. 128, 129, 155, 172 and 384.

Pictured to the left are the bases to a SPANISH LACE cracker jar and DAISY AND FERN syrup pitcher, showing the "marie" around the rim found on many Northwood items in blown opalescent glass. Below can be seen the polished pontil found on many of the earlier blown opalescent patterns made by Phoenix, Hobbs, La Belle and others. Shown here are a BLOWN HERRINGBONE pitcher and an OPAL SWIRL cruet.

Coinspot Patterns

COINSPOT

MAKERS: Virtually all factories, depending upon shape mold. The water pitchers must be an exact shape matchup to determine manufacturer.
OMN: Spot, Big Spot, Dot
COLORS: white, blue, green, yellow, amber, rubina, cranberry, amethyst and amberina
SHAPE MOLDS: too many to list here
REPROS: cracker jar, lamps, water pitcher, sugar shaker, tumblers, creamer, cruet, and syrup
RESEARCH NOTES: Obviously, this is one of the most produced patterns in all cranberry opalescent, and one of which to avoid reproductions. Beware of all handled items which use the reeded handle. However, the amber opalescent cruet in H6, Fig. 84 is definitely old and has a reeded handle. Avoid shapes which have been recently introduced, not originally made. A four piece table set is not known in this pattern (except for the RIBBED COINSPOT), which was limited to water sets and seasoning service items.

A cruet is known in amber opalescent, probably made by Phoenix or Hobbs. An amberina water pitcher in a possible Phoenix shape mold is also known.

West Virginia Glass Co. made this pattern in the same shape molds used for their POLKA DOT, a similar "dotted" pattern with colored, instead of opalescent white, dots lined up in perpendicular rows. Compare the Fig. 143, 144 and 208 water pitchers with the distinctive West Virginia cloverleaf crimped top. Compare also the hand lamps in POLKA DOT (Thuro1, p. 237) and COINSPOT (Thuro1, p. 273). Both have the same unique pressed handle.

Northwood made this pattern in his Ring Neck ane other shape molds, but no complete set is known. The pattern was also used by Northwood at his other factories, in different shape molds. This is unquestionably the most copied design in blown opalescent. See also RIBBED COINSPOT, which we also feel certain is Northwood.

Fenton made this pattern in a water set around 1907-1925 (with a pressed tumbler), but no cranberry opalescent. An iced tea pitcher (with ice lip) and tall tumbler were made in the late 1920's. A vase in COIN-SPOT was made in white and yellow opalescent in the late 1930's (see F2, p. 97). Do not confuse this pattern, which has the opalescent spots, for the similarly-named Fenton COIN DOT (introduced in the 1940's) which has the reverse colored dots on an opalescent background.

ITEMS KNOWN:
1. Water pitchers (several molds; 127, 129, 131, 132, 208, 248, 261)
2. Tumblers (130; many thick-walled reproductions)
3. Cruet (128—Indiana mold; 141—Buckeye jug; 142—Phoenix jug; 137—Ring Neck)
4. Syrup (193, 268—Ball-shaped; 195, 266—Ring Neck; 267—Nine Panel) others known
5. Finger bowls
6. Barber bottle (134—either Hobbs of Beaumont)
7. Master Berry bowl
8. Toothpick holder (Barrel shaped—probably Phoenix) others known
9. Sugar shaker (138—Ring Neck; 139—Nine Panel; 140—Wide Waist; 194—Bulb shape)
10. Water Bottle (278)
11. Oil Lamps (Northwood or West Virginia)
12. Lamp shades
13. Ice Bucket (N.I.)

REPRODUCTIONS (see also WRIGHT and FENTON reprints):
1. Water Pitcher (288)
2. Lamp (352)
3. Decanter (392)

JOURNAL QUOTE:
1/17/1889 P&GR
[Discussing Hobbs Glass Co. line]
... *The 328 water sets consist of five colors, pearl satin finish, crystal opal, sapphire opal, amber opal and pink opal. The outlook for the spring trade is excellent.* [Possibly Coinspot]

COINSPOT water pitcher in a Northwood shape, in rare cranberry color. It is also known in white and blue, and is sometimes trademarked (hard to find) with an N-in-a-Circle (from Wheeling factory), circa 1905

Another Northwood shape, this one from the Indiana, Pa., factory, in cranberry opalescent. Production was continued after the National glass merger in late 1899

This shape appears to be one by L.G. Wright, with this firm's distinctive reeded handle

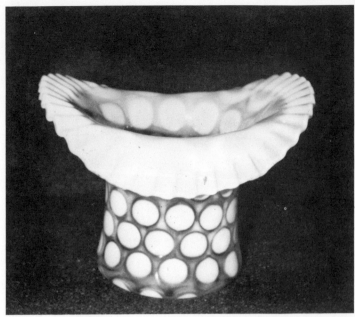

Yellow opalescent DOT OPTIC hat by Fenton Art Glass Co., circa 1939. This shape comes in varying sizes. The smaller size hat, in an OPAL SWIRL motif, was made by National Glass at the Indiana, Pa. and Buffalo, N.Y. Pan American Exposition factories

Cranberry COINSPOT cruet in Buckeye's jug shape, but with the "question mark" handle distinctive to several Northwood cruets. Another jug shape cruet was made, probably by Phoenix

COINSPOT cruet from RING NECK mold, made by Northwood at his Martin's Ferry factory

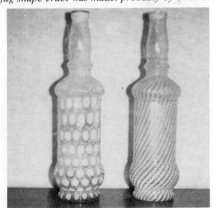

COINSPOT bar bottle next to same shape in what appears to be CHRYSANTHEMUM SWIRL. But is the latter merely a similar copy of the full table line? Bar bottles and straw jars are clearly described in Northwood's lines of 1889 and 1890

COINSPOT fount to hanging oil lamp, maker unknown

Yet another COINSPOT shape pitcher is shown in this collection of "shouldered" examples, all made at Indiana, Pa. factory by Northwood, National and Dugan

Whereas the tall iced-tea tumbler shape was made by Fenton in "Baby Coinspot" (called POLKA DOT in their 1955 catalogue), and in COINSPOT for L.G. Wright (in the 1950's-60's) and themselves (in the 1920's), this blue opalescent example is probably Imperial from the depression era. It is in their unusual Harding Blue color. See page 65 for OPAL STRIPE pattern in this Imperial entry into blown opalescent

COINSPOT AND SWIRL

MAKER: The Northwood Co., at Indiana, Pa., probably continued after National Glass merger
YOP: Circa 1898-1902
COLORS: white, blue and cranberry opalescent
SHAPE MOLDS: NORTHWOOD SWIRL, Indiana BALL-SHAPE syrup
REPROS: None

COINSPOT AND SWIRL is a very limited design found only in a syrup and cruet shape. It is unquestionably Northwood, copied by no other manufacturer

ITEMS KNOWN:
1. Cruet (133—Northwood Swirl mold)
2. Syrup (250—Ball-shaped)

COLLECTOR'S NOTES: The syrup jug is a most common piece in the blue opalescent color. It is extremely rare in cranberry opalescent.

COINSPOT AND SWIRL cruet from the same shape mold used for Northwood's PARIAN SWIRL cruet

RIBBED COINSPOT

MAKER: Probably Northwood at Martin's Ferry, although the shape of the pitcher is strikingly similar to the one used on Hobbs' STARS AND STRIPES
YOP: Circa 1888
COLORS: white, blue and cranberry opalescent
REPROS: None
RESEARCH NOTES: A "Spot" line is described in Northwood's line for 1888, and no other lines of COINSPOT can be matched in his early shapes except this one. It could be Hobbs, but catalogue evidence seems to refute this. A second pitcher with "fine ribs" is shown here.

ITEMS KNOWN:
1. Tumbler
2. Sugar lid (273)
3. Water pitcher (136)
4. Syrup (135)
5. Salt Shaker (371)
6. Sugar Shaker (196)
7. Celery (262)
8. Creamer

COLLECTOR'S NOTES: Very limited items have ever surfaced in this pattern: i.e. the tumblers, water pitchers, and the sugar lid. The finial of the sugar lid is identical to the sugar finial in the RIBBED OPAL RINGS pattern. One would assume that the remainder of the table set (spooner and butter) exists. However, none has been documented to date. There are no reproductions in this pattern.

JOURNAL QUOTES:
2/9/1888 P&GR

Capt. S. C. Dunlevy has a beautiful exhibit of the goods manufactured by the Northwood Glass Co., of Martin's Ferry , at the Monongahela House. They are chiefly blown lead goods and comprise tableware, water sets, flower holders, molasses cans, shades, gas globes, water bottles, finger bowls, hall globes, tumblers, casters, oil bottles, salt, pepper and oil cruets, and a general line of fancy glassware. The colors are most exquisite and include effects in satin finish, diamond, rib, spot, etc. This company's works are now in operation.

Blue opalescent COINSPOT pitcher from the same shape mold used on Northwood's CHRIST-MAS SNOWFLAKE (Fig. 178) "ribbed" pitcher. This could easily be confused for RIBBED COIN-SPOT, which has wider ribs

Rare RIBBED COINSPOT creamer in cranberry opalescent, not shown in color section of this book

RIBBED COINSPOT syrup pitcher. This is believed to be Northwood, but proof of manufacture remains elusive

RIBBED COINSPOT celery vase

OPALESCENT BULL'S EYE

MAKERS: Hobbs, La Belle, Phoenix, others
YOP: Circa 1885-1891
COLORS: white, canary, blue and cranberry opalescent
REF: *Thuro1, p. 239*
H2, Fig. 290
NOTES: This is similar to COINSPOT, but the spots are in slight relief, like large rounded hobs.

ITEMS KNOWN:
1. Hanging lamp shades
2. Hall lamps (cylindrical)
3. Gas shades (*H2, Fig. 578*)
4. Water bottle (*H2, Fig. 290*)
5. Assorted crimped bowls
6. Oil lamps

OPALESCENT BULL'S EYE water bottle. This is actually a variant of COINSPOT with the bumps or opalescent spots protruding slightly like enlarged hobs. These spots are perfectly flat on COINSPOT

Dot Patterns

POLKA DOT

MAKERS: West Virginia Glass Co., Martin's Ferry, O.; also produced by Northwood at Ellwood City and Indiana, Pa.
YOP: Circa 1893-1899
OMN: West Virginia's No. 203?
COLORS: white, blue and cranberry opalescent
REPROS: See L.G. Wright (Figs. 282, 291, 292, 294, 295, 301)
SHAPE MOLDS: WEST VIRGINIA OPTIC, FANCY FANS, others
RESEARCH NOTES: The water pitcher is known with the clover-leaf crimped top, both with and without pontil scars. I feel it is too soon to label those without pontil marks as Wright reproductions, as this particular shape mold is not an Indiana, Pa. shape. No water pitcher in this shape appears in any Wright literature I have located. Reproducing this shape would require the making of two expensive molds for the one pitcher, a larger spot mold and the shape mold. The same smaller spot mold was used by Wright for all their reproductions listed above. The melon-ribbed water pitcher is unquestionably Wright.

Fenton produced a quite different line they called POLKA DOT in the mid-1950's, but this is a variant of the old COINSPOT, with smaller "Baby Coinspots". See Figs. 321, 322, 324-327 for this pattern.

ITEMS KNOWN:
1. Water pitcher (143)
2. Tumbler
3. Cruet (155)
4. Salt shaker
5. Syrup (154, 156)
6. Finger bowl
7. Barber Bottle
8. Toothpick
9. Sugar shaker (201, 202, 277)
10. Oil lamps—several sizes
11. Celery Vase

COLLECTOR'S NOTES:

Reproductions abound in this pattern! Some using the identical old molds, and others redesigned—technically not reproductions—both providing great confusion to the collector. Fenton called their version of this pattern COIN DOT.

The old POLKA DOT water pitchers, cruets, barber bottles, and finger bowls have polished pontils. Most reproductions of these items do not have this identifying mark.

The old salt shakers, sugar shakers, and syrups do not have pontil scars.

The tumbler is by far the hardest to discern. Like the shakers and syrup, it will have a slightly rolled upper rim (often missing if chips have been polished out). But the best guide to new and old is the wieght. Old tumblers are "thin walled" and light in weight.

While L. G. Wright used a Melon ribbing on many of his re-issued pieces of Polka Dot, the Fenton Art Glass Co. remade the pattern so that the dots are staggered in alternate rows. The original POLKA DOT remains in perfect vertical and horizontal lines.

The L. G. Wright Company also makes a "creamer-size" pitcher which was never original in the pattern. It carries the taboo reeded handle.

Wright also used the Polka Dot pattern on the BEADED DRAPE shape in a miniature lamp. Remember, this shape of miniature lamp was never originally made in the POLKA DOT pattern. However, few of the Wright reproduced examples exist today. Many collectors add this piece to their cranberry opal collection because of its scarcity as a collectible.

The toothpick has never been reproduced.

JOURNAL QUOTE:
12/20/1893 CG&L
MARTIN'S FERRY, O. — The West Virginia Glass Co. have three complete lines of new goods and a lot of new specialties, all of which promise to be fast sellers. In the "Gem" ware there are four different effects, consisting of crystal, engraved, etched and cut No. 4, all finely finished. No. 203 is a pressed line, imitation of blown and there will be at least two decorations in this. It looks very much like blown. Another of the new lines is No. 204. This is blown and will be made in fancy colors, and there is quite a variety of it. The two new lines of novelties consist of sweetmeats, celeries, olives, etc. All of the above goods are entirely new and will be ready for the spring trade. . . .

2/22/1894 C&GJ
The West Virginia Glass Co. have gained an enviable reputation on account of the fine new goods they have on the market this season, and a local paper last week was prompted to say: "Their goods are made in a variety of pleasing colors and shapes, and are not excelled anywhere. Lot No. 203 is made in crystal, ruby-edged and gold-edged; No. 204 in crystal opalescent, in ruby, blue crystal, etched, engraved and cut; besides these they have a fine line of barbers' supplies, bottles, finger bowls, water and lemonade sets, etc., etc. In the 204 blown line the cream jugs have a strainer lip, which is sensible and practical, and is different from anything on the market."

POLKA DOT celery vase by West Virginia Glass. The shape mold used on this piece is the same one used on their OPTIC line

POLKA DOT from the FANCY FANS shape mold covered sugar in blue opalescent. This was introduced at Northwood's short-lived Ellwood City factory, and production was extremely limited. The shape molds were probably not moved to Indiana, Pa., but some examples from the spot mold are known to have been made at the latter site

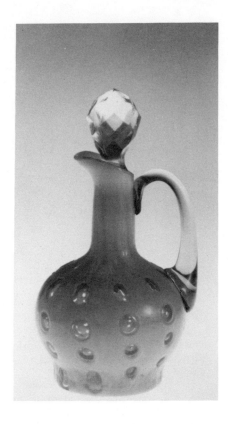

POLKA DOT night lamp from FANCY FANS shape molds, in blue opalescent

POLKA DOT water pitcher in West Virginia shape. This pitcher was made with and without a pontil scar on the bottom. Neither appears to be a reproduction. Apparently different finishing techniques were used

Rare unlisted POLKA DOT cruet from FANCY FANS shape mold, made by Northwood, shown here in blue opalescent

POLKA DOT barber bottle in melon-ribbed shape used by Beaumont around 1899 and reproduced by L.G. Wright from about 1950 to recent years. Since Beaumont is not known to have made POLKA DOT, this must be a Wright example

POLKA DOT salt shaker, sugar shaker and toothpick holder by West Virginia Glass Co., Martin's Ferry, Oh.

OPAL WINDOWS

MAKER: Originally by Hobbs Glass Co. (possibly designed by Beaumont), with additional later production at Beaumont Glass Co., Martin's Ferry; probably also made at Indiana, Pa. factory (see notes)
YOP: Circa 1889-1899
OMN: Dot, Hobbs' No. 333
REPROS: See L.G. Wright (Figs. 286, 287, 289, 290, 293, 297, 298, 299, 313, 350)
RESEARCH NOTES: This is actually a tiny "honeycomb" design, but the six-sided holes are melted out and appear to be round. Percy Beaumont apparently acquired some of the original molds from U.S. Glass (which owned the Hobbs factory) when he opened his own glassmaking factory in 1899. One catalogue page is suspiciously similar to an earlier one found in a Hobbs catalogue.

The Fig. 115 crimp-top pitcher was offered in an 1893 Butler Bros. catalogue. Hobbs was closed by U.S. Glass that year.

The large variety of shapes in the water pitcher, and the reproductions (probably from original spot molds) by L.G. Wright, have me convinced that a copy was made by Northwood or Dugan at the Indiana, Pa., factory, but this cannot be confirmed by any shape molds at this time.

ITEMS KNOWN:
1. Water pitcher (111, 115, 209)
2. Tumblers (114)
3. Miniature lamp (263—at least two shapes known)
4. Oil lamps (379—several shapes)
5. Finger bowl
6. Bitters bottle
7. Crimped bowl

COLLECTOR'S NOTES:

Do not confuse this with the WINDOWS SWIRL pattern, which is the same design blown into different shape molds. All of the shapes in the WINDOWS SWIRL pattern are oval in shape. Since there are limited pieces made in this pattern, let's discuss them separately: The water pitcher is known in two shapes—both are basically bulbous in shape. One has a square top, the other with a ruffled tri-cornered top. Both have clear (not reeded) handles. Both have polished pontils.

The water pitcher has been reproduced. The reproduction is also bulbous in shape. It has a plain handle and has no pontil scar.

The tumbler also has been highly reproduced. Here again, with most all reproduced opalescent tumblers, the weight is the key factor. Light weight glass is old—reproduction tumblers tend to have thicker walls and are heavier in weight.

The finger bowl can be found in both the new and the old form—unfortunately, like the tumblers, they are difficult to tell apart. The weight is the determining factor.

Wright expanded the range of this pattern, making a few items that were never originally produced: a two handled vessel that resembles an open sugar, a creamer size pitcher (both of these items carry the reeded handle), and a cruet! No old plain WINDOWS cruet has ever been found.

WINDOWS pattern pitchers in two different shapes made by Hobbs and U.S. Glass (Factory H), from 1889-1893. Beaumont Glass Co. also made the square-top shape in 1899

Our "OPALESCENT" Blown Water Set.

The Great and Matchless Home Decorator.

Heretofore the rich opalescent colors could not be included in any popular priced sets, but we have made arrangements for a large quantity, and are enabled to include all the most expensive in this beautiful selection; such as Ruby Opalescent, Crystal Opalescent, Old Gold, Crystal Sapphire and Sapphire Opalescent. *All strictly "firsts."* Each set comprises 1 half gallon jug, 2 tumblers to match, 1 slop bowl to match, and 1 metal tray. 12 sets (2 each of the above colors) in a bbl. Sold only by bbl.

......Order here,   Price per Set, 58c.

1893 Butler Bros. catalogue listed this WINDOWS pattern water set in white, blue and cranberry opalescent, and plain colors of crystal, blue and amber ("Old Gold"). The finger bowl is called a slop bowl here

Opalescent WINDOWS pattern night lamp by Hobbs Glass Co., from circa 1891 catalogue. This line was continued after U.S. Glass merger

WINDOWS pattern ruffled bowl in frame from circa 1902 Rockford Silver Plate Co. catalogue. This bowl was probably made by National's Northwood factory at Indiana, Pa., based on a shard from the base of this bowl found at the plant site and based on Wright reproductions

WINDOWS SWIRL

MAKER: Hobbs Glass Co., Wheeling, W. Va.
YOP: Introduced in 1889
COLORS: white, blue and cranberry opalescent
SHAPE MOLD: No. 326 "Hobbs' Swirl" (also used on FRANCES WARE line)
OMN: Hobbs' No. 326
REPROS: None

ITEMS KNOWN:
1. Water pitcher (113)
2. Tumblers (112)
3. Cruet (122)
4. Salt shakers (125)
5. Syrup (123)
6. Butter (116)
7. Covered Sugar (118)
8. Creamer (119)
9. Spooner (117)
10. Finger bowl

11. Master Berry Bowl
12. Sauce
13. Sugar shaker (126)
14. Mustard pot
15. Celery vase (120)
16. Toothpick holder (124)

COLLECTOR'S NOTES:

A pattern that was made in a variety of shapes (including the complete table set), which has never been reproduced! The WINDOWS SWIRL pattern is always oval in shape—even the tumbler (which remains the roundest piece) tends to have an oval shape. You will easily recognize this tumbler, for it has a wide flat (not swirled) upper edge.

JOURNAL QUOTE:
1/17/1889 P&GR

Wheeling—Goods that will be hard to excel are the three new lines of the HOBBS GLASS CO. They are just out and are "rippers." The numbers are 326 [FRANCES WARE SWIRL mold], 327, and 328. The former is made in ten effects, namely, crystal, crystal opalescent, sapphire, ruby, these four colors in satin finish, decorated No. 7 and "Frances." In these they have a full line of table ware such as nappies, bowls, sugar sifters, molasses jugs, tumblers, pitchers, water bottles, finger bowls, celeries, (boat and straight) salts, peppers, mustards, toothpicks, castors, also shades, oil bottles, etc. The shape is oval, entirely new, and all the articles named are made in this shape except tumblers. . . .

WINDOWS SWIRL syrup pitcher

BIG WINDOWS

MAKER: Buckeye Glass Co., Martin's Ferry, Oh.,
YOP: Circa 1887-1889
OMN: No. 527 "Dew Drop"?
COLORS: white, blue and cranberry opalescent; same molds made in speckled glass and opaque colors
SHAPE MOLDS: BUCKEYE LATTICE, REVERSE SWIRL shape molds used
REPROS: Similar to Fenton's COIN DOT
RESEARCH NOTES: Similar to, and previously confused for Hobbs' WINDOWS SWIRL (see *H3*, Figs. 333-334). No toothpick holder is known, and the pattern is very rare, indicating short-lived production.

SHAPES KNOWN:
1. Butter (214)
2. Creamer (215)
3. Covered Sugar
4. Spooner
5. Sugar Shaker (275)
6. Syrup (252)
7. Water pitcher

8. Tumblers
9. Barber bottle
10. Oil lamps

COLLECTOR'S NOTES:

The water pitcher was made in the same shape mold as that used on BUCKEYE LATTICE. The rest of the set was made in a swirled mold used to make REVERSE SWIRL. The pattern so closely resembles the WINDOWS SWIRL and BUCKEYE LATTICE patterns, that it is often mistaken for them. The OPAL HONEYCOMB design, which is similar, has spots that are even larger, distinctively six-sided. Also keep in mind that the WINDOWS SWIRL shapes are entirely different—true WINDOWS SWIRL is oval, not round in shape.

JOURNAL QUOTE:
6/23/1887 P&GR

At the BUCKEYE GLASS WORKS business is still good, with encouraging prospects for the future. The season has been a very prosperous one and the management is well pleased over it. Only one furnace, the large 15-pot one, has been in use but this has always worked to perfection and has turned out a large amount of ware, very little of which will be left unsold when the bars are drawn. There are now many fine fancy goods in the sample rooms than ever and a visit to it will pay any person. A line of goods is ready for the fall trade which ought to meet with a quick sale. The number of the new plain and opalescent dew drop table set is 527 [BIG WINDOWS?], and it is a pretty thing. The decorated vase lamps, six patterns with decorated shades to match, are very handsome. In Venetian thread ware [SWIRL or STRIPE?], plain and decorated, they have a water set, new shapes in oil and vinegar bottles, new shapes in molasses jugs and lamp chimneys, salts, lamps in blue, white and canary, and other articles. These Venetian goods are something the Buckeye has not been making and are very neat and the decorations show to good advantage on them. . . .

BIG WINDOWS master berry and syrup pitcher in cranberry opalescent, made by Buckeye Glass Co. in same molds as used on their REVERSE SWIRL line

BIG WINDOWS water pitcher from shape mold used on BUCKEYE LATTICE water pitcher. No pitcher from the REVERSE SWIRL mold is known in BIG WINDOWS

This bitter bottle is believed to be BIG WINDOWS. which is actually a Honeycomb design (as are Plain and Swirled WINDOWS) with the six-sided sections rounded out from melted detail.

Floral Patterns

DAISY AND FERN

MAKERS: Northwood at Ellwood City and Indiana, Pa.; Production continued by National and Dugan at Indiana, Pa. factory; West Virginia Glass at Martin's Ferry (in OPTIC mold) and possibly Beaumont
YOP: Circa 1894-1904
SHAPE MOLDS: APPLE BLOSSOM, NORTHWOOD SWIRL, WEST VIRGINIA OPTIC
RESEARCH NOTES: Shown in a November, 1894 *C&GJ* Northwood (Ellwood City) advertisement in the ball-shaped pitcher set (Fig. 17). Northwood apparently retained the molds or reintroduced the pattern when he opened his own Indiana, Pa. factory. After he left in December, 1899, the pattern was kept in production, first by National Glass (appeared in a 1903 BB catalogue) and then by Dugan Glass.
REF: *PGP3, p. 8*
PGP2, p. 14
H1, p. 31
H2, p. 43
H3, p. 22
H6, pp. 25, 97, 98

ITEMS KNOWN:
1. Water pitcher (15—Northwood Swirl; 17—Ball Shape; 18—Shouldered mold)
2. Tumblers (16A—Northwood Swirl; 18B—Tapered)
3. Cruet (23—Northwood Swirl)
4. Salt shaker (Northwood Swirl)
5. Syrup (192—Northwood Swirl; also NINE PANEL; W.V. OPTIC)
6. Finger bowl
7. Bitter bottle (211)
8. Berry bowl (21—Northwood Swirl)
9. Sauce (20—Northwood Swirl)
10. Toothpick holder (Northwood Swirl)
11. Spooner/caster insert (26—Apple Blossom mold; 239—N. Swirl)
12. Sugar shaker (24—Wide Waist; 204—N. Swirl)
13. Rose bowl (small size)
14. Vase (210)
15. Covered Sugar (238—N. Swirl)
16. Creamer (240—N. Swirl)
17. Butter (N. Swirl—N.I.) Probably exixts
18. Night Lamp (APPLE BLOSSOM mold—see *Smith1, p. 136*) See also *Smith 2, p. 79*

REPRODUCTIONS:
1. Tumbler (306)
2. Assorted lamps (353, 355)
3. Apothecary jar (279)
4. Pickle caster insert (280)
5. See listing below (see also Wright reprint)

COLLECTOR'S NOTES:
All pieces of DAISY AND FERN that are in either the "Northwood Swirl" or "Apple Blossom" mold have never been reproduced. A covered butter dish must have been made, as the other three pieces to the table set exist. Pieces in the "Melon Rib" mold are probably a re-made copy of the pattern (although some old examples do exist) and should be purchased with care. Beware of all items which have a reeded handle. Avoid all items which were never originally made (the apothecary jar and lamps in particular).

The spooner mold for the APPLE BLOSSOM pattern was used as a shape mold for a caster insert in DAISY AND FERN (Figure 26). But since no butter dish, creamer or covered sugar is known in this variant, we believe it to be an occasional piece.

Items made with silver attachments: pickle caster (using spooner mold), spooner (pickle caster insert), wedding bowl (brides bowl)

The molds for this pattern were purchased in the late 1930's by L.G. Wright. This pattern was massively reproduced by Fenton for the Wright firm. All items in yellow opalescent are new. All items with satin finish are reproductions.

L. G. Wright Glass Co. has unfortunately re-made and added to the DAISY AND FERN pattern to the extent that many collectors of old glass shy away from the pattern. The list of items recently made is as long or longer than the original production. The only items that have escaped being reproduced are the salt shakers, finger bowl, and toothpick holder.

Reproduced shapes: rose bowl (small and large), milk pitcher, water pitcher, tumblers, cruet (round and oval), syrup, barber bottle (Melon Rib and round mold), cracker jar, lamps (GWTW ball shades, Hurricane lamps, oil lamps), sugar shaker (nine panel mold), creamer, and handled basket, mantel lustres.

Reproduced additions to the pattern (items originally never made) are the oil lamps, large rose bowl, creamer, cylindrical shape vessel called a spooner (more like a pickle castor insert), milk pitcher (larger than a creamer but smaller than a water pitcher), a wedding bowl (the shape and size of a brides basket), the large covered cracker jar, and a handled basket (in two sizes).

This long running and extensive reproductions have virtually made this pattern feared by many opalescent glass collectors. The items made in the N. Swirl, West Virginia OPTIC and Apple Blossom shape molds are the only reliable old pieces. While there are old examples of plain DAISY AND FERN, only purchase them from reliable dealers who will guarantee their age.

JOURNAL QUOTE:
1/9/95 CG & L
The Northwood Glass Co., of Ellwood City, Pa., represented by John G. Anderson, have their exhibit in room 73. No. 91 [DAISY & FERN?] is a full line in opalescent in three colors—flint, blue and pink, very showy as well as neat in shapes. No. 182 comes in two colors, crystal and ruby flash, also in gilt and gilt with enamel decorations, being entirely new and the largest line the company ever made. The gilt ornamentation harmonizes well with the flowers in enamel [PANELLED SPRIG]. This line is made in two patterns, flint and ruby. There are half a dozen new lemonade sets, the decorations on which, it is worth remarking, are a great improvement on all that have preceded them in this line. There is a new molasses can, of unique shape, and half a dozen new salts and peppers. These with new crimped bowls, a large assortment of night lamps, both new and old, fancy baskets, sugar sifters and the usual line of novelties complete a very attractive display.

1/18/1900 C&GJ
The new lines displayed at the National Glass Co.'s showrooms now number about eighteen. The McKee factory has five, headed by the "Vulcan", a rich, elegant pattern a little on the order of their magnificent "Apollo" of '99. The Northwood has one new line and several new creations in

*pieces and sets. This factory's ware is all opalescent and opal, and is very artistic, dainty, delicate and ornamental. **The opalescent is in a number of elegant tints — pink, canary, green, blue, etc.** — and is more or less engraved. The "Nautilus" opal possesses striking beauty in its shapes and decorations. . . .*

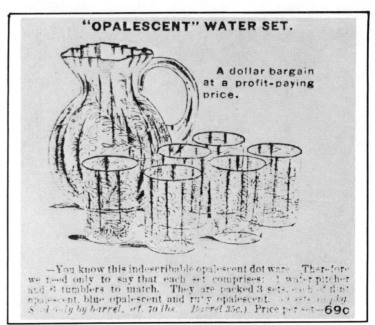

"OPALESCENT" WATER SET.

A dollar bargain at a profit-paying price.

—You know this indescribable opalescent dot ware. Therefore we need only to say that each set comprises: 1 water pitcher and 6 tumblers to match. They are packed 3 sets, each of flint opalescent, blue opalescent and ruby opalescent.
S...d only by barrel, at 70 lbs. Barrel 35c.) Price per set—**69c**

Rare DAISY AND FERN syrup pitcher in the NINE-PANEL shape, made by Northwood National Dugan at Indiana, Pa.

An 1899 Butler Bros. included this DAISY AND FERN water set (by Northwood) which could be retailed for $1.00 (69 cents wholesale). It was listed in white, blue and cranberry opalescent.

The set was again shown in 1903, selling for 66 cents wholesale (this time made by National Glass at the same factory).

DAISY IN CRISS CROSS

MAKER: Beaumont Glass Co., Martin's Ferry, O.
YOP: Circa 1899-1901
COLORS: white, blue, cranberry and green opalescent
REPROS: None

ITEMS KNOWN:
1. Water pitcher *(PPG 2, p. 94)*
2. Tumblers
3. Syrup (19)

COLLECTOR'S NOTES:
Another limited design pattern in the fantastically beautiful cranberry opalescent DAISY IN CRISS CROSS. It has never been reproduced and is difficult to find.

Cranberry opalescent DAISY AND FERN water pitcher in unusual shape, from the collection of Dugan family

DAISY AND FERN pitcher in green opalescent, a rare color, in a shape made by Northwood and his successors at Indiana, Pa.

Rare DAISY AND FERN bitters bottle, probably Northwood, but some of this pattern was also made by West Virginia Glass

Beaumont's DAISY IN CRISS CROSS syrup pitcher

FLORAL EYELET

MAKER: Probably Northwood/National/Dugan at Indiana, Pa.; Reproduction water sets by L.G. Wright
YOP: Circa 1896-1904
COLORS: White, blue and cranberry opalescent
REPROS: Water set by L.G. Wright in blue opalescent
RESEARCH NOTES: The water pitcher in cranberry has never been confirmed, but undoubtedly exists. A very rare tumbler is shown in color in this book (Fig. 221). The attribution is based on the reproductions by L.G. Wright, probably made from original molds acquired at Indiana, Pa. Production

Blue opalescent reproduction FLORAL EYELET pitcher, which L.G. Wright Glass Co. called DAISY AND EYE DOT

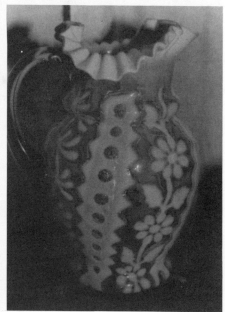

Blue opalescent FLORAL EYELET water pitcher probably made originally at Indiana, Pa. Production must have been very limited

by Northwood must have been very limited as the pattern is very rare today. Note the similarity of the "eyelet" to the design on Consolidated's CRISS-CROSS.

ITEMS KNOWN:
1. Water Pitcher
2. Tumbler (221)

OPALESCENT FERN

MAKERS: West Virginia Glass Co. (designed by Beaumont); Beaumont Glass Co.; Model Flint Glass Works (no cranberry known)
YOP: Circa 1894-1902
SHAPE MOLDS: W. V. OPTIC, BEAUMONT SQUARE-TOP pitcher, MELON-RIB barber bottle
COLORS: white, blue and cranberry opalescent; yellow by Model Flint
RESEARCH NOTES: The finial on the covered butter (Fig. 260) and the base seems to match the Hobbs SEAWEED butter, indicating possible additional production at HOBBS (where Beaumont worked earlier). A similar ball-shaped finial is found on RIBBED OPAL LATTICE, but it is slightly different.
REPROS: By Fenton (1952-54) in their own molds.

ITEMS KNOWN:
1. Water pitcher (144—West Virginia; 145—Beaumont; a third shape by Model Flint Glass with unusual crimped top; a fourth ice-lip pitcher by West Virginia)
2. Tumblers (152)
3. Cruet (151)
4. Salt shakers (389)
5. Syrup (148)
6. Sugar shakers (149) 2nd shape known
7. Toothpick holder (150—W. V. OPTIC)
8. Butter (260—wrong base)
9. Covered Sugar (lid only—390)
10. Creamer (N.I.)
11. Spooner (388)
12. Master Berry Bowl (223)
13. Sauce (222)
14. Celery vase (259)
15. Finger bowl
16. Mustard pot
17. Bitter Bottle (147, 398—latter also made by Beaumont)

COLLECTOR'S NOTES:
A most attractive cranberry pattern which can be found with or without the opalescent fern. The pattern is free of reproductions and remains an attractive pattern to collect.

TRADE QUOTE:
1/17/1894 CG&L
. . . *There is a large line of barbers' supplies, bottles, finger bowls, etc. Water*

*and lemonade sets appear in opalescent colors and some of the old goods are also seen here. **The cream and ice jugs of No. 204 blown line are quite different from anything heretofore made in glass. These creams and jugs have a strainer lip, which is practical and sensible.** The West Virginia is out for business and will keep right along with the procession.*

1/31/1894 CG&L
The new illustrated catalogue of the West Virginia Glass Co., of Martin's Ferry, Ohio, is now ready and an examination of its pages reveals a wealth of beauty in color and design. In No. 203 ware are shown molasses can, sugar sifter, salts, tumbler, pitcher, finger bowl, set, handled celery, handled olive, handled pickle, plates—4 to 10 inch—blown oil, nappies—4 to 9 inch—, tooth pick, custard; all the foregoing in gold edge and ruby edge; and oil, molasses can, tumbler, sugar sifter and salts of the same pattern in ruby as well. No 201 comprise sweet meats of leaf pattern, 5 to 9 inch, in gold edge, ruby edge and green. In No. 204 there are oils, tooth pick, molasses can, celery, salts, sugar sifter, blown set, nappies, bowls, tumblers, finger bowl, gal. pitcher and ice pitcher, in ruby optic, crystal optic, ruby opalescent and crystal opalescent [OPALESCENT FERN]. No. 206 is ruby ware, plain and engraved, and of it are shown pitchers, blown tumblers, finger bowls and custards. They have No. 206 also in crystal, plain and engraved. No. 2 line of barber bottles and bowls is in blue opalescent, ruby opalescent and crystal opalescent and No. 3 is another line of the same goods with amber or ruby label and plain or wreath engraving.

Assortment of OPALESCENT FERN from an 1894 Montgomery Ward catalogue. Not the original cut glass stopper in the cruet. The detail on the engraving of the toothpick is inaccurate

Yellow opalescent FERN tankard pitcher, in a shape attributed to Model Flint Glass Works (National) at Albany, Ind. This shape is not known in cranberry

Cranberry opalescent FERN pitcher with clover-leaf top. This shape has never been reproduced

JOURNAL QUOTE:
11/15/1902 CG&L

There is a real novelty in a lemonade set shown here from the Northwood factory. This set and some new molasses cans are among the newest things on the display tables of Frank Miller, the New York representative of H. Northwood & Co. The lemonade set refered to has a jug of graceful shape, but it is the decoration which,at once attracts the eye. Its flower and foliage seem to stick right out, although the relief is not high. The effect is secured by the opalescent tint of the relief, which upon the various backgrounds of canary, flint, blue and pink, is most striking. It is certainly a novelty and shows that Mr. Northwood knows how to produce original effects. Still, he usually did do that. The molasses cans have nothing new in the shapes, but they are revivals of one of the best selling shapes we ever had [the tall tapered shape?], and, made as the Northwood factory is making them, in dainty colors, why shouldn't they sell better than ever they did?

Blue Opal Ware.

A new pattern, just out, made in fancy colored glass in blue opal. It is of a rich deep blue and the raised work gives it the optic effect. This pattern is destined to be one of the most popular ever produced in glass of this character.

54925 Blue Optic Table Set, consisting of the four pieces as illustrated above. Per set.......$1.00

54926 Blue Optic Half-gallon Pitcher; new shape and good value for the money asked for it. Price.................$0.65

54927 Blue Optic Half-pint Tumbler. When used with pitcher makes an elegant water set. Per dozen.....$1.35

54928 Blue Optic Finger Bowl; a very convenient article for the dinner table. Each.................$0.20 Per dozen...........2.16

The line called "Blue Opal Ware" is in West Virginia's OPALESCENT FERN pattern. Note the butter base is different from that shown on page 98. The creamer has an unusual open pouring spout. From an 1894 Montgomery Ward catalogue

OPAL POINSETTIA

MAKER: H. Northwood & Co., Wheeling, W.V.; possibly also made earlier, reportedly by Hobbs, but more likely at an earlier Northwood factory
YOP: Circa 1902
COLORS: white, blue, canary, green, rubina and cranberry opalescent; also marigold carnival; white with blue rim
REPROS: None

SHAPES KNOWN:
1. Water pitcher (174, 177—Two other shapes known)
2. Tumblers (pressed and blown varieties)
3. Syrup (see *H3, Fig. 405-D*—no cranberry known)
4. Large crimped bowl (185)
5. Sugar shaker (See *H3, Fig. 227*—no cranberry known)

COLLECTOR'S NOTES:

Limited pieces are contained in this highly collectible pattern. The tall tankard is highly sought after by collectors. The tumblers come in both a pressed and blown variety. Cranberry opal tumblers are very rare and come in only the blown variety. Collectors prefer the blown tumbler, because the opalescence adheres to the pattern.

The large bowl is ruffled, which was made to be placed in a silver-plated holder, but was advertised without holder in the early wholesale catalogues.

Both the syrup and sugar shaker are extremely rare and hard to find pieces in this pattern. No reproductions have ever plagued the POINSETTIA pattern.

Cranberry OPAL POINSETTIA pitcher by Northwood at Wheeling. Two other shapes are shown on the next page

Rubina OPAL POINSETTIA crimped salad bowl

A second shape in OPAL POINSETTIA, also known in decorated colored glass, by Northwood at Wheeling

A third shape in OPAL POINSETTIA, also by Northwood at Wheeling. This same shape is known in decorated carnival and colors. A fourth shape is shown as Fig. 177 in color, and a fifth shape is also reported but unconfirmed

ROSE ONYX

MAKERS: Dalzell, Gilmore & Leighton, Findlay, Ohio
YOP: 1889
OMN: FLORADINE?
COLORS: shiny and satin cranberry opalescent, plain cranberry; assorted onyx colors
REPROS: none

RESEARCH NOTES: This seems to be the only cranberry opalescent pattern made by Dalzell, Gilmore & Leighton. Thus, it is listed as a minor manufacturer of cranberry opalescent, but its contribution is the most expensive of all patterns found in this color. The rare non-satin version of this pattern is shown in *H2, Figs. 292-293.*

1. Butter
2. Covered Sugar (257)
3. Creamer
4. Spooner
5. Mustard (258)
6. Water pitcher
7. Toothpick holder
8. Celery vase
9. Sugar Shaker
10. Syrup pitcher
11. Salt shaker
12. Assorted vases
13. Pickle caster
14. Berry Bowl
15. Sauce
16. Finger bowl
17. Cruet
18. Tumbler

COLLECTOR'S NOTES:

One of the most difficult cranberry opal patterns to find—and one of the most expensive to purchase—is Findlay's ROSE ONYX. Art glass collectors highly regard this limited production, and often refer to the satin variety as "Raspberry Onyx". We know that the Findlay ONYX line was made in many pieces (water set, table set, celery vase, berry set, syrup, cruet, and toothpick). The only reported cranberry opal glossy pieces are the spooner and open sugar shown in *H2.* However, I have seen the entire table set in the satin finish.

If you would be fortunate enough to find an example of this pattern for your collection, it would certainly be worth adding it at most any cost.

JOURNAL QUOTES:
P&GR (circa 1889)

*Dalzell . . . show a magnificent assortment of ware . . . But what we want to call special attention to are their new lines of colored ware. The first of them, which they call **FLORADINE** ware, is in two colors, ruby and autumn leaf, with the patterns elegantly traced on the exterior. The effect is extremely rich. In this they make sets, bottles, jugs, celeries, molasses cans, finger bowls, sugar dusters, 8-in bowls, and several other articles. The other, the "Onyx" ware is still more beautiful and there is nothing in glass on the market to surpass it. The colors of this are onyx bronze and ruby and the pieces are all white-lined. Like the Floradine, the pattern is impressed on the exterior in graceful forms, and only for the shining surface the ware would look more like fine china than glass . . . The above firm have the exclusive rights to make these goods being the originators of them and they have their privileges secured by patents.*

1/31/1889 C&GJ

*The Dalzell, Gilmore & Leighton Co. opened the new year with some of the handsomest novelties ever produced in this country, which are destined to have an immense run. Among these is something entirely new, being **ruby and opalescent**, with raised figures of flowers and leaves, producing an effect of great beauty, but which is simply indescribable. It is a great relief to those who have grown tired of seeing polka dot and plain knobs. A patent has been applied for to cover the method of production and the new process is capable of a large variety of forms and designs that must necessarily render it the best selling thing in tableware.*

SCOTTISH MOOR

MAKER: Unknown, but possibly West Virginia Glass
YOP: Circa 1890-1900
REPROS: None
COLORS: white, blue, cranberry and light amethyst opalescent; also rubina
RESEARCH NOTES: See pitcher, next page.

SHAPES KNOWN:
1. Water pitchers (265—another shape shown here)
2. Tumbler
3. Cruet (N.I.—has reeded handle)
4. Cracker jar (N.I.)
5. Celery vase (*H2, p. 49. Fig. K*)

SCOTTISH MOOR tumbler in rare cranberry opalescent. Probably made by West Virginia Glass, year unknown

This amethyst opalescent SCOTTISH MOOR water set has the clover-leaf top shaped pitcher used by West Virginia Glass on their FERN and POLKA DOT patterns. This firm made blown amethyst (non-opalescent) in their MEDALLION SPRIG

OPAL DAFFODILS

MAKER: H. Northwood Company, Wheeling, W. Va.

YOP: Circa 1905-08

COLORS: white, blue, cranberry, yellow and green opalescent

REPROS: none

NOTES: A single tumbler has been found in the rare cranberry. The attribution is based on a variant of the flower found on a marked oil lamp. The syrup pitcher I reported in *H2* was probably confused for the POINSETTIA by the person who reported it to me. Thus, the shapes in the pattern are limited to the water set and the lamp.

SHAPES KNOWN:
1. Water Pitcher
2. Tumbler
3. Oil lamp (signed Northwood)

This pattern is known as OPALESCENT DAFFODILS and is probably Northwood. A variation of the flower is found on an oil lamp whose stem is trademarked with the Wheeling N-in-a-Circle.

Geometric Patterns

OPALESCENT DIAMONDS

MAKER: Probably made at either Phoenix or Northwood's Martins Ferry factory; other possibilities—Hobbs, Brockunier, Geo. Duncan & Sons or La Belle
YOP: Circa 1884-1889
SHAPE MOLDS: Compare Figs. 224 and 228
COLORS: white, blue, cranberry and rubina opalescent
REPROS: none
RESEARCH NOTES: OPALESCENT DIAMONDS is quite different from most blown opalescent in that the diamond portion of the pattern is opalized, the exact reverse of LATTICE, which has the diamond-work surrounded by opalescence. The attribution is speculative, based on Fig. 199. The Fig. 224 tankard may have been made from a retooled mold used earlier for Fig. 228, causing the uniform increase in dimensions as new detail is carved into the mold. The sugar shaker in this pattern is from a mold previously thought to have been Hobbs, but now believed to be Phoenix.

The crackled finish cruet is identical in shape and finish to one made by George Duncan & Sons Co., Pittsburgh (see *H3, p. 75*), but I am unable to confirm this company made blown opalescent. However, we do know they made art glass colors like peach-blow, cranberry, rubina and rubina verde. Perhaps this was their experimentation with opalescent.

The shape of this cruet is fairly standard, so any final attribution must await further investigation and additional shapes. It is difficult to imagine more than one factory made this unusual opalescent treatment. The extremely light opalscence makes this pattern less desirable than most other patterns. See also K6, pl. 101 cruet.

ITEMS KNOWN:
1. Water pitcher (224; see also *H2, p. 49, Fig. F*)
2. Tumblers
3. Cruet (225—a Duncan or Hobbs shape?: 234—decorated; 270)
4. Sugar Shaker (199—COLORATURA mold)

Rubina OPALESCENT DIAMONDS cruet with enamel decoration, probably made by Phoenix Glass Co. when Northwood was associated with the firm, circa 1884-85

Blue opalescent OPALESCENT DIAMONDS pitcher with unusual simulated crackled shape mold used. This appears to match one made at Hobbs, Brockunier in the 1885 period

COLLECTOR'S NOTES:
Very limited production of a quality cranberry opalescent pattern. The glass gives as appearance of a "crackle-type" finish. Both the cruet and water pitcher carry polished pontils. The tumbler is light in weight. The pattern has never been subject to reproductions.

OPAL HERRINGBONE
(Ribbed and Plain)

MAKER: A possible Northwood design made at Phoenix (also in Mother-of-Pearl), and also his own Indiana, Pa., factory.
YOP: Circa 1885 (plain) to 1902 (ribbed)
COLORS: white, blue, canary and cranberry opalescent; also in cased Mother-of-Pearl satin glass (sometimes shiny)
SHAPE MOLD: Fig. B (Front cover)—also in satin glass
REPROS: none
RESEARCH NOTES: Shards in white, blue and yellow opalescent were found at Indiana, Pa. factory site

ITEMS KNOWN:
1. Water pitchers (226—Northwood; B—Phoenix)
2. Tumblers (232—also made with smooth surface)
3. Cruet (227—Northwood; 235—Phoenix)
4. Syrup
5. Crimped salad bowls (mostly in yellow, sometimes with speckled glass rim treatment)

COLLECTOR'S NOTES: Very beautiful and limited pattern in cranberry opalescent. This pattern has never been subject to reproductions. Only one syrup has surfaced to date—a very rare squatty jug.

Blue OPAL HERRINGBONE ruffled bowl, probably Northwood at Indiana, Pa. This has been found with a cranberry speckled edge, used at both Northwood and later at Jefferson

Cranberry OPALESCENT HERRINGBONE (Ribbed) pitcher and tumbler by Northwood at Indiana, Pa. The top of the pitcher is identical to the DAISY AND FERN pitcher on page 48, but the bottom portion of the mold appears to have been altered when the ribs were smoothed out of the mold for the later Dugan production

OPALESCENT HONEYCOMB

MAKERS: Either Hobbs or Phoenix Glass Co.; also Northwood at Indiana, Pa.
YOP: Circa 1884-1888
COLORS: blue, white, amber and cranberry opalescent known; also known in cased glass colors; rainbow color
SHAPE MOLD: square-top squatty pitcher
REPROS: none in this variant
RESEARCH NOTES: Some pieces of BIG WINDOWS, which is also a Honeycomb design with rounded "dots", can be confused for this pattern. OPALESCENT HONEYCOMB is known in amber opalescent (see Fig. 274). The reeded handle and color are distinctively Phoenix, although this color was also made at Hobbs.

ITEMS KNOWN:
1. Water pitcher (231; see also *H2, p. 49, Fig. G*)
2. Tumblers (153, 242)
4. Cracker jar
5. Barber bottles (2 shapes known)
6. Small juice pitcher (274)
7. Juice glass (Champagne tumbler)
8. Oil lamp (*Thuro1, p. 236*—probably BIG WINDOWS)
9. Syrup pitcher (Ball shape—*H3, Fig. 147*)

JOURNAL QUOTE:
1/17/1889 P&GR
(Reviewing display of Hobbs Glass Co.)
   . . . *The 328 water sets* [OPALESCENT HONEYCOMB?] *consist of five colors, pearl satin finish, crystal opal, sapphire opal, **amber opal** and pink opal. The outlook for the spring trade is excellent.*

Rare green OPALESCENT HONEYCOMB oil lamp, possibly English. The fount fits inside a hollowed vase base

OPALESCENT SWASTIKA

MAKER: Dugan Glass Co., Indiana, Pa.
YOP: Circa 1907
OMN: Unknown
SHAPE MOLDS: Indiana Ball-shape syrup, FILIGREE "Diamonds & Clubs" tankard
COLORS: white, blue, green and cranberry opalescent
RESEARCH NOTES: This extremely rare pattern was one of the last patterns made in cranberry opalescent until Steuben's and Fenton's revival of the color in the 1930's.

SHAPES KNOWN:
1. Water pitcher (2 shapes)
2. Tumbler (2 types)
3. Syrup (198)

JOURNAL QUOTE:
1/12/1907
   Walter G. Minnemeyer states that the price of diamonds has increased 40 per cent and that the quality of their ware, the Diamond D, increased 100 per cent . . . This year they have originated another new style of ware, Filigree Gold and Filigree Silver glass. These lines are in three colors, viz ivory, green and Royal blue. In vases these lines have an additional color, viz, Ruby. The Filigree work is most perfectly executed and an examination of it is necessary in order to convince yourself that it is not inlaid work. It is a unique and handsome production and has met with universal favor. This line runs in a half a dozen different sizes of steins, wine sets, decanters, whisky sets, tobacco jars and four-piece sets.

Green OPALESCENT SWASTIKA tumbler on DIAMONDS AND CLUBS shape mold. This pattern is limited to a water set and a syrup pitcher, and was made by Dugan Glass Co. at Indiana, Pa.

Lattice Family

CONSOLIDATED CRISS-CROSS

MAKER: Fostoria Shade & Lamp or Consolidated Lamp & Glass Co., Fostoria, Oh.
YOP: Circa 1893-94
COLORS: White, cranberry and rubina opalescent—satin or glossy finish
OMN: "Cable"?
REPROS: None
NOTE: The only opalescent pattern made by this company, which was started by former Hobbs, Brockunier staff, including Nicholas Kopp and Lucien Martin. The butter bases on Figs. 49 and 53 are different, but both are probably original. Fig. 49 has a frosted base with a polished pontil. Fig. 53 is the same base found on the FLORETTE and GUTTATE butters.

ITEMS KNOWN:
1. 8⅝" Water pitcher (43, 47)
2. 3⅝" Tumblers (46)
3. 4½" Cruet (52, 54)
4. 3½" Salt shakers (44)
5. Syrup (255)
6. Butter (49, 53)
7. Covered Sugar bowl (48)
8. Creamer (51)
9. Spooner (50)
10. Finger bowl
11. Master Berry Bowl
12. Sauce
13. Mustard pot (254)
14. Celery vase
15. Toothpick holder (45)
16. Sugar Shaker (200)
17. Ivy Ball (247)

COLLECTOR'S NOTES:
Considered one of the most sought after and highly collectible patterns in cranberry opalescent, Consolidated's CRISS CROSS is one of the most expensive designs. The pattern has never been reproduced and is available in a variety of shapes. Because of the vast color differentiation, it is difficult to keep a consistency in the cranberry shade. The criss-crossing in the pattern is sometimes blurred together or tends to swirl instead of remaining completely vertical. This pattern must be considered one of the finest ever produced in cranberry opalescent.

If indeed this pattern was made by the earlier Fostoria Shade and Lamp Co. (predecessor to Consolidated at same factory), then this pattern should be called simply OPAL CRISS-CROSS.

But we have no proof yet that this was the pattern trade journals referred to as "Cable". Shown here in a syrup pitcher and oil cruet

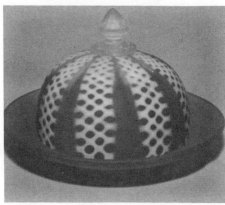

Cranberry opalescent butter dish in CONSOLIDATED'S CRISS-CROSS

BUCKEYE LATTICE
(Formerly Bubble Lattice)

MAKER: Buckeye Glass Company, Martin's Ferry, Ohio
YOP: Circa 1888-90
COLORS: white, blue, yellow, rubina and cranberry opalescent; in shiny or satin finish
MOLD: The BUCKEYE BUBBLE shape mold, also used on decorated milk glass
REPROS: None

ITEMS KNOWN:
1. Water pitcher (92)
2. Tumblers
3. Cruet (97)
4. Salt shakers (372)
5. Syrup (197)
6. Butter
7. Covered Sugar (256)
8. Creamer (380)
9. Spooner (381)
10. Finger bowl
11. Master Berry bowl
12. Sauce

13. Sugar shaker (100)
14. Toothpick holder (103)
15. Celery vase
(See also OPAL LATTICE notes.)

Cranberry opalescent BUCKEYE LATTICE sugar bowl. one of several variants of the motif made by a number of companies

OPAL LATTICE

MAKERS: Northwood Glass Works, Martin's Ferry, O. and The Northwood Company, Indiana, Pa., possibly continued by National and Dugan after 1900; also made earlier at Phoenix Glass Company and also possibly La Belle Glass Co., Bridgeport, O.
YOP: Circa 1884 to 1902
OMN: Diamond, Diamond Optic
SHAPE MOLDS: QUILTED PHLOX (108), RIBBED PILLAR (110); see also RIBBED OPAL LATTICE, BUCKEYE LATTICE
REPROS: See Figs. 283, 296, 317, 334, 395
NOTES: Shards confirm some of this pattern was made at Indiana, Pa. The Fig. 94 pitcher is a shape mold from there. The Fig. 228 satin tankard may be from Northwood's earliest factory (described below), but it has the reeded handle and light pink color found on many Phoenix pieces.

Sometimes WINDOWS can look like tight lattice-work, but it is actually tiny little honeycombs which have melted out.

ITEMS KNOWN:
1. Various water pitchers (228—satin tankard; 94 & 95—Northwood)
2. Tumblers (109)
3. Ruffled salad bowl (391)
4. Salt Shakers (108)
5. Cruet (102—Indiana Oval mold)
6. Spooner-caster insert (110—RIBBED PILLAR mold)
7. Various lamp shades
8. Sugar bowl (241—lid only)
9. Sugar shaker (H2, Fig. 372)

COLLECTOR'S NOTES:
LATTICE— the crossing of slanted diagonal lines to make "diamond-like" designs. Opalescent LATTICE assumes that it is the only design in or on a piece of glass. Most of the pieces that contain this design are "bulbous" in shape: therefore, the name by which it was previously known, "BUBBLE" LATTICE. Because there are so many different bulbous shapes carrying the opalescent lattice design, the name has been changed to the known maker, BUCKEYE LATTICE. This variant and RIBBED OPAL LATTICE are the only two known complete lines in this opalescent motif. The occasional items are listed here under this generic heading, with a variety of unlisted shape molds a distinct possibility. For example, the OPAL LATTICE design may turn up in a NINE PANEL sugar shaker or syrup shape mold.

There have been some remakes of the pattern—but none that I feel should confuse the collector. For instance, the cruet was made by Fenton in the 1950's—it is 7 inches tall (one inch taller than the standard cruets); an Ivy bowl, a cracker jar, and a few different shape and size vases—are things that were never originally made.

The L. G. Wright Glass Company commissioned Fenton to produce a creamer and possibly a two-handled open sugar. Both of these carry the taboo reeded handle.

Too often collectors find pieces that are not listed in the original production—and far too often they assume they have an "old rarity", rather than a "new re-make"!

JOURNAL QUOTE:
2/9/1888 P&GR
*Capt. S. C. Dunlevy has a beautiful exhibit of the goods manufactured by the Northwood Glass Co., of Martin's Ferry , at the Monongahela House. They are chiefly blown lead goods and comprise tableware, water sets, flower holders, molasses cans, shades, gas globes, water bottles, finger bowls, hall globes, tumblers, casters, oil bottles, salt, pepper and oil cruets, and a general line of fancy glassware. The colors are most exquisite and include effects in satin finish, **diamond,** rib, spot, etc. This company's works are now in operation.*

The shape of this rubina OPAL LATTICE pitcher (with reeded handle) appears to match one used by Jefferson Glass Co. for their SWIRLING MAZE pattern (Fig. 162 in color). However, this appears to be an earlier production item, maker unknown

Blue OPAL LATTICE crimped bowl, probably Northwood at Indiana, Pa., circa 1900

Cranberry opalescent pitchers in OPAL LATTICE by (left) L.G. Wright, circa 1950, and by Northwood, circa 1898

RIBBED OPAL LATTICE

MAKER: Probably Northwood at Martin's Ferry, but could be slightly earlier La Belle, as the ribbed design is so similar to RIBBED PILLAR and the shape molds used on RIBBED COINSPOT and RIBBED OPAL RINGS
YOP: Circa 1886-1889
COLORS: white, blue and cranberry opalescent
OMN: Diamond
REPROS: None
RESEARCH NOTES: Do not confuse for the similar OPAL LATTICE in the RIBBED PILLAR mold.

ITEMS KNOWN:
1. Water pitcher (93)
2. Tumblers (105)
3. Cruet (96)
4. Salt shakers (106)
5. Syrup (251)
6. Butter (99)
7. Covered Sugar (245-lid only)
8. Creamer
9. Spooner (N.I.)
10. Master Berry (N.I.)
11. Sauce (N.I.)
12. Toothpick holder (see H1, Fig. 199)
13. Sugar shaker (98; two sizes made—see also H3, Fig. 251)
14. Celery Vase (104)

JOURNAL QUOTE:
2/9/1888 P&GR
Capt. S. C. Dunlevy has a beautiful exhibit of the goods manufactured by the Northwood Glass Co., of Martin's Ferry, at the Monongahela House. They are chiefly blown

RIBBED OPAL LATTICE creamer, probably Northwood in 1888

lead goods and comprise tableware, water sets, flower holders, molasses cans, shades, gas globes, water bottles, finger bowls, hall globes, tumblers, casters, oil bottles, salt, pepper and oil cruets, and a general line of fancy glassware. The colors are most exquisite and include effects in satin finish, diamond, rib, spot, etc. This company's works are now in operation.

COLLECTOR'S NOTES:
Another highly collectible and beautiful pattern. While the set contains a table set, the collector will find this an extremely difficult one to put together. Another "safe" pattern—this one has never been subject to reproductions.

Rare short sugar shaker (two sizes are known) in cranberry RIBBED OPAL LATTICE

Rococo Patterns

ALHAMBRA

MAKER: Unknown
YOP: Circa 1894-1900
COLORS: white, blue, yellow and cranberry opalescent
REPROS: none
NOTES: The syrup jug was reported to me several years ago with a drawing, not an actual photograph. It is a round bulbous bowl with an ornate metal top and handle combination (as in *H3, Fig. 208*). The glass portion could have been formed from the rose bowl. The water pitcher must have been made, but as yet has been unconfirmed.

ITEMS KNOWN:
1. Rose Bowl
2. Syrup Jug (N.I.)
3. Tumbler

White opalescent ALHAMBRA rose bowl. This shape was made by Northwood at Indiana, West Virginia Glass and by Jefferson. The limited number of known shapes leaves an attribution inconclusive

ARABIAN NIGHTS pitcher which is similar to a shape mold used by Beaumont (K7, pl. 60). The shape is also similar to one used on DAISY IN CRISS CROSS water pitcher (VCG2, p. 94).

ARABIAN NIGHTS

MAKER: Probably Beaumont Glass Co., Martin's Ferry, Oh.
YOP: circa 1900-1904
COLORS: white, blue, canary and cranberry opalescent
REPROS: none
REF: *H2, p. 42*
NOTES: The attribution is highly questionable. The shape mold on the water pitcher matches that on DAISY IN CRISS CROSS. The crimp is one used by Northwood, Dugan, Jefferson and Beaumont.

ITEMS KNOWN:
1. Water Pitcher (159)
2. Tumblers (160)

COLLECTOR'S NOTES:
A facinating and highly embellished pattern which apparently was made only in a water set. The pattern has never been reproduced and maintains great respect among cranberry opalescent collectors.

BUTTONS AND BRAIDS

MAKER: Jefferson Glass Co., at Steubenville, Oh.; similar copy made by Fenton around 1910, but no cranberry
YOP: circa 1902-1910
COLORS: white, blue, green and cranberry opalescent
REPROS: none in recent years
REF: *F1, pp. 31, 103*
NOTES: The Fenton version of this pitcher, not made in cranberry, has five "backward C's" extending from each scroll. The Jefferson version has seven closer extensions. Frank L. Fenton designed for Jefferson at the time the earlier version was introduced. He apparently copied this design, and the COINSPOT pattern, when Jefferson discontinued their production of fancy glassware around 1908.

Blue opalescent ALHAMBRA tumbler, maker uncertain. No water pitcher has yet been confirmed to accompany this tumbler. The shape mold used on it may help determine the manufacturer

ITEMS KNOWN:
1. Water Pitcher
2. Tumblers
3. Vase (Fenton)
4. Fish bowl (Fenton)

COLLECTOR'S NOTES:

The tumblers in this pattern are either blown or pressed. The blown examples are of lighter weight and have opalescence in the pattern detail, while the pressed variety carries opalescence at the top of the tumbler. Both are old. Most collectors prefer the blown variety.

The cranberry opalescent tumblers are always blown. The cranberry color was never made in pressed glass.

BUTTONS AND BRAIDS water pitcher in cranberry opalescent by Jefferson. A variant of this pattern was made by Fenton, with seven "Backward C's" in the design instead of the five regular C's on the Jefferson original. The Fenton version was never known made in cranberry, and the spot mold was later used for a few novelty items around 1930

OPALESCENT SEAWEED

MAKERS: Complete set by Hobbs, Brockunier & Co., circa 1891; some shapes made later by Beaumont Glass Co., circa 1900; reported additional production by Northwood, probably at Wheeling location
YOP: circa 1890-1902
REF: *K7, pls. 58, 62, 63*
SHAPE MOLD: The same one used on Hobbs' BULBOUS BASE (sugar shaker, cruet, toothpick, syrup and salt shaker); Northwood Multi-Ribbed rose bowl
NOTE: The square-top pitcher water set, three bitter bottles (tapered, round and sqaure), oval cruet and a finger bowl were reintroduced about 1899 by designer Percy Beaumont (who earlier probably designed the pattern when working for Hobbs). The inclusion of a full line of this pattern in a

Northwood catalogue has been reported to me, but never proven. However, this seems possible. A rose bowl in yellow opalescent SEAWEED in a Northwood multi-ribbed mold is known. Perhaps Northwood did indeed acquire a few old Hobbs molds when he purchased the Wheeling factory in 1902. This certainly would explain the BULBOUS BASE sugar shaker in Northwood's distinctive purple slag.

ITEMS KNOWN:
1. Water pitcher (27—Hobbs shape; 31—Beaumont shape)
2. 3⅞" tumblers (41)
3. Cruet (38, 42—Bulbous Base; Oval shape by Beaumont—none known in cranberry)
4. Salt shakers (37—Bulbous Base)
5. Syrup (40—Bulbous Base)
6. Butter (33—on plain clear blown base with polished pontil)
7. Covered Sugar (32)
8. Creamer (35)
9. Spooner (34—3½" high)
10. Barber Bottle (3 shapes—29, 30)
11. Master Berry Bowl
12. Sauce
13. Sugar shaker (39—Bulbous Base)
14. Celery Vase (28)
15. Night lamp (264)
16. Toothpick holder (36—Bulbous Base)
17. Oil lamps (Hobbs—see *Thuro2, p. 104*)
18. Rose Bowl (multi-ribbed mold)
19. Pickle caster (188—spooner insert)

COLLECTOR'S NOTES: Another outstanding cranberry opalescent pattern which comes in both glossy and satin finishes. The pattern was also made in a complete table set. The water pitcher, cruet, and oil lamp can be found in several shapes. Probably one of the most unique cruet shapes I have ever seen is the SEAWEED pattern in the HOBBS SWIRL mold. Several pieces are difficult to find—the toothpick holders and sugar shaker in particular—and must be considered very rare. No reproductions have been made in this pattern.

OPALESCENT SEAWEED night lamp by Hobbs Glass Co., continued by U.S. Glass

OPALESCENT SEAWEED covered sugar in rare satin finish

Cranberry OPALESCENT SEAWEED syrup (in BULBOUS BASE shape), celery vase and satin finish cruet, all by Hobbs Glass Co. The celery vase is similar in shape to the one known in

SCOTTISH MOOR, but Percy Beaumont worked for Hobbs and could have copied the shape for West Virginia's line

Cranberry OPALESCENT SEAWEED pickle caster on ornate frame. Hobbs supplied inserts for metal holders to a number of different silverplate firms. including Pairpoint. Meriden and Wilcox

OPALESCENT SEAWEED bitters bottle which was made by both Hobbs and Beaumont (possibly from original molds), circa 1890-1899

SPANISH LACE
(OPALINE BROCADE)

MAKER: The Northwood Company, Indiana, Pa., with possible later production after National Glass takeover in late 1899
OMN: OPALINE BROCADE; BROCADE
YOP: Introduced in 1899
SHAPE MOLDS: UTOPIA OPTIC table pieces, The NINE-PANEL tankard and sugar shaker, the RIBBON TIE salt shakers
REPROS: handled basket by Fenton in

limited edition; Fenton pressed variation of pattern in opaque glass colors (no cranberry)
NOTE: The unusual applied "twig" finial is the same one found on Northwood's UTOPIA OPTIC decorated tableware. This same shape mold was used on a line of decorated milk glass, with scenic trasfer decoration or hand-painted "delft" decoration. While the cruet and the syrup have "reeded" handles, they are original, and should not be thought of as reproductions. The night lamp is shown in *Smith1, Fig. 471*. This shape mold is the same one used by Northwood on his Delft decorated milk glass line (*Smith1, p. 150*) and in decorated colored glass for the UTOPIA OPTIC (*Smith, Fig. 470*).

ITEMS KNOWN:
1. Water pitcher (Three or more styles; 2, 4, 5)
2. Tumbler (3; 3⅝" tall)
3. Cruet (14; 5¾" tall; reeded handle)
4. Salt shakers (11; RIBBON TIE mold; 3¼" tall)
5. Syrup (13; BALL-SHAPE shape mold; reeded handle)
6. Butter (6)
7. Covered Sugar (8)
8. Creamer (9)
9. Spooner (7)
10. Finger bowl
11. Barber Bottle
12. Master Berry Bowl
13. Sauce (crimped)
14. Sugar shaker (12; WIDE WAIST mold)
15. Wine decanter (1; only one known)
16. Night lamp
17. Water Bottle
18. Perfume
19. Rose bowl
20. Celery vase

Items made with silver attachments:
1. Jam jar
2. Cracker jar
3. Brides Basket (using Master Berry Bowl)

Items never made:
1. Toothpick holder

JOURNAL QUOTES:
1/12/1899 CG&L
[Ad for Northwood on Intaglio, Opaline Brocade and Venetian.]

1/12/1899 CG&L
Harry Northwood, the glassmaster, is present himself in Room 62, and assisted by a staff of salesmen, has been kept busy showing buyers his handsome new lines. The trade has annually come to look to Northwood for blown and pressed lines of glassware which, in design, finish and conception, are of a higher artistic merit than the ordinary or general run of glassware pattern, and Harry has never disappointed the trade in this respect, and this year is no exception to the rule. This year three original lines are shown, each distinct from the other, which are briefly described as Intaglio, in ivory and gold, and green and gold; Opaline Brocade [SPANISH LACE], in four colors, including pink, and Venetian [UTOPIA

SPANISH LACE water bottle in blue opalescent

SPANICH LACE covered butter in yellow opalescent with yellow base. The cranberry covered butter has a white pressed base

Rare green opalescent SPANICH LACE sugar shaker in NINE PANEL shape

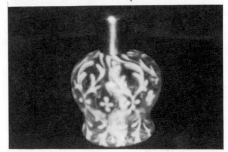

This perfume in SPANISH LACE was probably formed from the base to the night lamp. It is white opalescent

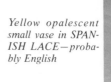

Yellow opalescent small vase in SPANISH LACE—probably English

OPTIC], in enamel colors and gold, and in three colors, ruby, blue and green.

Yellow opalescent round vase in SPANISH LACE. This is definitely English, but is it an an original design or a copy of Northwood's. We simply do not know who was first

SPANISH LACE tankard pitcher in RIBBON TIE mold. This shape is similar to the shorter NINE PANEL tankard

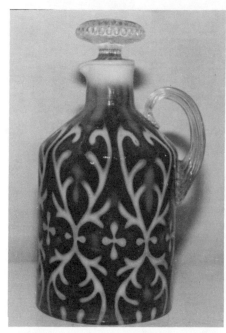

Extremely rare SPANISH LACE wine decanter, the only example reported to date

Green opalescent SPANICH LACE pitcher with star-crimp top, one of several shapes in which this pattern pitcher is found

SPANISH LACE syrup pitcher in Indiana Ball-shape (UTOPIA) mold

SPANISH LACE yellow opalescent sugar shaker in WIDE WIAST (UTOPIA) shape

SPANISH LACE barber bottle, very rare, and never reproduced

This jam jar was a special blown shape supplied to silver-plate manufacturers. See the sugar bowl at right

Another round blown blank with attached silver plate rim, handles and lid. This may have been sold by Northwood, but more likely was marketed by a silver-plate manufacturer

Stripe Patterns

STRIPE

MAKERS: Northwood, Buckeye, Beaumont, Jefferson, Nickel, others
YOP: Circa 1886-1904
COLORS: white, blue, canary, cranberry and rubina opalescent
SHAPE MOLDS: Northwood's AURORA (Ring Neck); NINE-PANEL;
others AKA: OPALESCENT STRIPE, WIDE STRIPE (a variant)
OMN: Venetian Thread, Venetian Rib
REPROS: The syrup jug has been highly reproduced. The handle of the repro is plain (not reeded) which often fools the novice. However, the jug has two rings at the top—while the old one has only one ring around the neck. Also many items were made by Fenton during the 1920's, 30's, and 1952-62, in their own shapes.
NOTES: This basic design of vertical stripes was made by many factories, including many examples from England (see *Smith*, p. 210-212, Fig. 511 and 519). Color and shape molds are essential in naming manufacturers for each variant. No table set has been reported to date, although it is possible. See also WIDE STRIPE.

The maker of the Fig. 87 cruet and Fig. 203 sugar shaker, probably the same company, remains a mystery. These shape molds match no other attributable pattern. I believe it is either Buckeye at Martin's Ferry or the American Glass Co., at Anderson, Ind., but this is only a guess. Whoever made the sugar shaker probably made the STRIPE oil lamp shown in *Thuro2, p. 117*.

The STRIPE or WIDE STRIPE pattern made at Nickel-Plate, continued by U.S. Glass, is usually more milky pink in color, with the opalescence bleeding into the cranberry. However, the Fig. 212 oil lamp, with a Nickel-Plate base, has a darker color. Perhaps this firm made the two items mention in the previous paragraph.

A similar STRIPE pattern was definitely made by Buckeye. A November, 1887 trade journal describes their "Venetian rib chimneys". These are shown in a February, 1888, lamp reprint in *Thuro2, p. 123*.

The shape of the Fig. 91 barber or bitters bottle matches one known in DAISY AND FERN, and is probably Northwood. The Fig.

88 cruet is in a mold for which no maker is known. It could be La Belle, Phoenix or American Glass Co.

ITEMS KNOWN:
1. Water pitcher (75—RING NECK mold) Many others known
2. Tumblers
3. Cruets (87, 88, 382; others known)
4. Salt shakers (various shape molds)
5. Syrup (89—RING NECK; others)
6. Finger bowl
7. Sugar shaker (187, two others p. 64)
8. Two caster sets (187; *H2, p. 98*)
9. Assorted Oil lamps (212—many others)
10. Lamp shades
11. Miniature lamps (various)
12. Large crimped bowl (387)
13. Assorted Jefferson vases
14. Celery vase (Northwood—see p. 64)
15. Toothpick Holder (90—RING NECK)
16. Barber bottle (91—Northwood shape)
17. Wine decanter
18. Assorted smaller tumblers, shots

REPRODUCTION NOTES:
The barber (or bitters) bottle has also been reproduced by L.G. Wright (Fig. 302). I know of no old barber bottle in the Wright "Melon rib" mold—which appears to be a copy from an old original by Beaumont (see catalogue *H3, p. 61*). This shape bottle is known in FERN (Fig. 398), a pattern which has not been reproduced by Wright. I have also studied a collection of old barber bottles which included this same melon-rib mold in POLKA DOT, SWIRL and DAISY AND FERN. These last three patterns have been much reproduced, but these bottles were acquired many years ago and showed all indications of being old when compared to known L.G. Wright examples. The difference between the mold on the Beaumont original and the Wright reproductions is minimal.

The Pilgrim Glass Corp. produced some white opalescent small pitchers (from 5" to 7" tall) in the 1960's, but these should fool no one.

JOURNAL QUOTES:
6/23/1887 P&GR
At the BUCKEYE GLASS WORKS busi-

ness is still good, with encouraging prospects for the future. The season has been a very prosperous one and the management is well pleased over it. Only one furnace, the large 15-pot one, has been in use but this has always worked to perfection and has turned out a large amount of ware, very little of which will be left unsold when the bars are drawn. There are now more fine fancy goods in the sample rooms than ever and a visit to it will pay any person. A line of goods is ready for the fall trade which ought to meet with a quick sale. The number of the new plain and opalescent dew drop table set is 527, and it is a pretty thing. The decorated vase lamps, six patterns with decorated shades to match, are very handsome. In Venetian thread ware, plain and decorated, they have a water set, new shapes in oil and vinegar bottles, new shapes in molasses jugs and lamp chimneys, salts, lamps in blue, white and canary, and other articles. These Venetian goods are something the Buckeye has not been making and are very neat and the decorations show to good advantage on them.

Yellow opalescent STRIPE water pitcher with square-top made by a number of firms. This is probably Nickel-Plate, without the usual WIDE STRIPES associated with their line

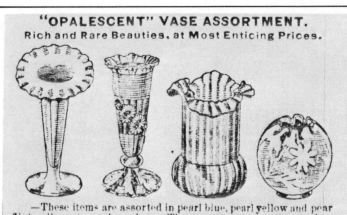

"OPALESCENT" VASE ASSORTMENT.
Rich and Rare Beauties, at Most Enticing Prices.

—These items are assorted in pearl blue, pearl yellow and pear flint—all most popular colors. The assortment comprises ½ doz. of each of the following:

Opalescent Fancy Vase—6 inches high, flaring extremity.
Wide Flare, Lily Top Vase—6½ in. high, assorted in 3 shapes.
Large Venetian Striped Flare Top Vase—6 inches high, also suitable for celery.
Flower Bowl—Rose bowl shape, bent in, scalloped upper rim.
(Total, 6 doz. in bbl. Sold only by bbl. Bbl. 25c.)

Price per dozen—**82c**

From 1899 Butler Bros. catalogue—this assortment included a 6" vase in Opalescent STRIPE (this shape mold also used for SPANISH LACE), and a rose bowl in DAISY AND FERN

Cranberry opalescent STRIPE by Northwood in his RING NECK mold used at Martin's Ferry, circa 1890

Yellow opalescent STRIPE pitcher, tumblers, slop bowl and pressed tray (the latter previously thought to be BEATTY SWIRL). I now believe this to be Northwood based on the similarity of the pitcher to RIBBED COINSPOT, and a known pressed tray to accompany a COINSPOT set. However the shape of the pitcher also matches Hobbs' STARS AND STRIPES

Opalescent STRIPE syrup and sugar shaker, maker unknown. These are possibly from John F. Miller's short runs at either American Glass Co. or Model Flint Glass Works. Neither shape is known, however, in cranberry, indicating the latter.

Blue opalescent wine decanter in Opalescent STRIPE by Beaumont Glass Co., Martin's Ferry, circa 1899

The shape mold used on this syrup seems to be the same one used by Northwood on his Opalescent POINSETTIA syrup (H3, p. 52). However, the ribs on the mold match Nickel-Plate's ROYAL pattern design. This could be just a coincidence

Blue opalescent STRIPE sugar shaker in NINE-PANEL shape

WIDE STRIPE

MAKERS: Originally in England; Probably Phoenix at Monaca or Northwood at Martin's Ferry; also by Nickel-Plate Glass at Fostoria, Ohio
YOP: Circa 1889-1892
COLORS: cranberry, blue, green and white opalescent
REPROS: Fenton from the late 1930's (see reprint) in their own shapes; also Imperial
OMN: Nickel's No. 84 and 94
NOTES: This version of the STRIPE motif has slightly wider and fewer stripes running vertically. The difference between STRIPE and WIDE STRIPE is sometimes minimal, and a matter of opinion. However, the possible Northwood/Phoenix version has decidedly massive wide stripes. The attribution of Fig. 230 is based on the similarity of color to the LEAF MOLD sugar shaker shown on the cover of *H2*. The color of pink and white are distinctively separated on both items.

ITEMS KNOWN:
1. Water pitcher (230—Phoenix/Northwood; also by Nickel)
2. Tumbler (402)
3. Cruet (271)
4. Toothpick holder (*H1*, Fig. 213—Nickel)
5. Salt shaker (368)
6. Sugar Shaker (206—Nickel)
7. Syrup (two shapes—see *H3*, Figs. 294-295)
8. Assorted lamps

COLLECTOR'S NOTES:

Another extremely limited production pattern. While there are other WIDE STRIPE pieces—such as several miniature lamps—few shapes have the secondary "Diamond Mold". These are believed to be Northwood. Compare the color to that on the LEAF MOLD sugar shaker in *H2*, Fig. 375. Both the water pitcher and the cruet in this pattern have polished pontils. WIDE STRIPE on the Diamond mold remains a "safe" pattern to collect.

Fenton used the WIDE STRIPE motif on a line of gift ware in the late 1930's and mid-1950's which they called WIDE RIB.

Blue opalescent WIDE STRIPE pattern, maker unknown. The reeded handle is definitely found here on an old pitcher. This could be Phoenix or La Belle

JOURNAL QUOTE:
1/14/1891 CG&L

*The Nickel Plate Glass Co., of Fostoria, Ohio, have their interests attended to by Mr. W. A. Rolf in Room 152. They show a large assortment of goods. The new pattern, No. 77, "Royal" ware is a handsome one and they have a full line of it, . . . The company also manufacture **a line of blown and pressed opalescent ware, among which are pitchers of several sizes, molasses cans, sugar sifters, salts, peppers, oil bottles, water bottles, finger bowls, etc.**; also staples, such as tumblers, goblets, ales, beer mugs, berry sets, lamps, etc. . . .*

The pitcher is not made with opalescent stripes in the same manner as the other glass shown in this book. It is made in the same manner as "rainbow" colored art glass, with intermittent panels of color, in this case opaque white and cranberry. See also Figs. 271 and 230 in color. These are similar to the color found on the cover of H2 (the rare LEAF MOLD sugar shaker)

This pitcher is similar to Nickel's WIDE STRIPE, but is actually from Imperial Glass Co.'s limited opalescent production in the 1930's

Blue opalescent WIDE STRIPE cruet, maker unknown

Swirled Patterns

OPALESCENT SWIRL

MAKERS: Virtually all factories featured in this book. Attribution depends upon the shape mold used. The manufacturers of "sets" include Hobbs, Brockunier (their No. 325 Ware) and Nickel-Plate (their No. 80 and 90 Ware), the latter started by former Hobbs personnel. Much also came from England. Also made by Steuben in ORIENTAL POPPY line in 1930's
YOP: Circa 1885-1910
COLORS: white, blue, green, yellow, rubina and cranberry opalescent; rare in amber opalescent; sometimes decorated
OMN: Venetian Thread, Spiral Optic, Twist
REPROS: Many by L.G. Wright and Fenton (see reprints)
RESEARCH NOTES: OPAL SWIRL was probably made with the same spot mold as OPAL STRIPE, with the opal stripes leaning at an angle. The same technique was used to change BLOWN OPAL DRAPERY to BLOWN TWIST.

Perhaps the different companies should be used in the pattern names for the many SWIRL variants, but in some cases this may prove to be impossible. Hobbs and Beaumont used the same molds, and the same may be true of Northwood and Dugan. Thus all variants are grouped under the generic name SWIRL below.

A round jug is known in this pattern, shaped like Fig. 229, possibly made to go with one of the juice glasses shown on front cover.

The Fig. 246 straw jar matches the shape mold used by Beaumont in 1899-1900. However, it could have been made earlier by Hobbs or even Northwood (a straw jar is described in his displays for 1889). The finial on this jar is not broken off. It simply was never attached.

The Fig. 86 sugar shaker was made as late as 1909, appearing in Butler Bros. catalogues. Thus it is probably Dugan, the only factory making this color that year.

The Fig. 79 square-top pitcher matches shapes by Hobbs, Nickel-Plate and Beaumont. The Hobbs cranberry is usually darker with the opalescent swirls more distinct, sometimes even raised somewhat. The Nickel-Plate cranberry is usually more "pink"

with the opalescence less defined.

Jefferson made the pattern in a water set, vases, rose bowls, crimped bowls and possibly a sugar shaker.

ITEMS KNOWN:
1. Water pitchers (77, 79—see *VCG2, p. 111*) others known
2. Tumblers (76)
3. Cruet (78, 83, 216, 382)
4. Salt shakers (367)
5. Syrup (85)
6. Finger bowl
7. Barber bottle (91)
8. Sugar shaker (81, 82, 86, 207)
9. Toothpick holder (84—Nickel)
10. Water bottle
11. Master berry
12. Sauce
13. Rose bowl (401)
14. Bar bottle
15. Custard cup
16. Celery vase (80—Hobbs)
17. Covered cheese dish
18. Spooner
19. Lamp shades (189)
20. Oil lamps (several sizes)
21. Night lamp (378—also some made in England)
22. Straw holder with lid (246)
23. 2¼" shot glass (front cover)
24. 3¾" juice glass (front cover)
25. Melon-rib bowl
26. English punch set (405-407—back cover)
27. English vases (356, 358)

COLLECTOR'S NOTES:
Reproductions include: small size creamer (never originally made), the cruet (which has a reeded handle), a barber bottle (in the Melon-ribbed Mold), a sugar shaker (in the Nine Panel mold), the water pitcher (with reeded handle), the tumbler (the weight is the most significant difference), and a variety of vases, decanters, and shakers (all in shapes never originally made). The pattern was one of the most prolific made. It was made by several companies. The two most recognized companies are the Hobbs, Brockunier and the Nickel-Plate glass companies. It will help most collectors to know which pieces of these swirl patterns were made where. The shape will help inform you as

much as anything. On some pieces you will find a fire polished pontil (such as the cruet and barber bottle), these can definitely be attributed to Hobbs. For as extensive a list as was originally produced, one will find pieces of this pattern hard to come by as soon as you have completed your water set.

This SWIRL motif was used by Fenton since 1939. Examples of their shapes shown in this book are Figs. 314, 316, 319, 320, 323, 330, 335, 374, 375, 404.

This is one of the cranberry opalescent patterns which has been hurt by the reproductions on the market. Perhaps this can be rectified by a more knowledgeable buying public. All pieces which have the raised opalescent swirls are definitely old, made by Hobbs. All have polished pontil scars (see Fig. 78, 79, 216).

This is another pattern which Hobbs used in a silver plated frame—primarily the cruets and salt shakers—to provide the Victorian table with a castor or seasoning set.

JOURNAL QUOTE:
7/19/1888 P&GR (partial)

. . . of the Buckeye Glass Co. holds . . . In lamps there are opal, turquoise, crys . . . opalescent; night lamps with globes and decorat . . . ed with glass and metallic feet, parlor lamps, from . . . all fine art decorations and with real bronze trim . . . so a large variety of gas and kerosene globes in . . . will as **hall cylinders in big spot, diamond, Venetian** *. . . specialties are decorated molasses jugs, casters, . . . shakers, and a volume of fancy articles for holiday . . . they have a full line of thin blown flint ware, engraved . . . in a great variety of styles.*

This blue opalescent SWIRL lamp is one of many known made in several sizes. All are carefully covered in the books by Catherine Thuro

Blue opalescent MELON RIB SWIRL large berry bowl

This OPALESCENT SWIRL pitcher in white appears to be in a Beaumont shape, similar to that used on his DAISY IN CRISS CROSS

198

Cranberry opalescent glass is rarely decorated, but here is a beautiful example in the short ball-shape which could have been made by either Hobbs, Phoenix, La Belle, Northwood or even in England

A February, 1909, Butler Bros. catalogue included this rather late entry into blown opalescent sugar shakers, probably made by Dugan Glass Co. It was offerred in white, blue and green opalescent for 92 cents per dozen wholesale

This satin finish white opalescent SWIRL pitcher has an unusual blue reeded handle, and is probably Phoenix

This punch set is shown on our back cover and has unusual light blue feet, handles and finial. It is probably English, with the most likely attribution being Stevens & Williams of Stourbridge

Cranberry opalescent SWIRL punch cup or custard cup, maker unknown. It does not match the shape of the Hobbs Glass Co. custard cup

ITEMS KNOWN:
1. Water pitchers (58, 60)
2. Tumblers (59)
3. Cruet (68)
4. Salt shakers (57A-B) Two types
5. Syrup (74)
6. Butter (71)
7. Covered Sugar
8. Creamer
9. Spooner (70)
10. Master Berry bowl (220)
11. Sauce (219)
12. Toothpick holder (69)
13. Sugar shaker (73)
14. Celery vase
15. Oil Lamp with brass foot (*Thuro1, p. 235*) A similar pattern?
16. Bar Bottle (190) Similar?
17. Straw Holder (Fig. F—cover) Similar?
18. Finger bowl (p. 71)
19. Custard cup

COLLECTOR'S NOTES:
This is a highly collectible pattern—One of the few cranberry opalescent patterns to have a complete table set. There have been no reproductions in this pattern. All pieces were made in both glossy and satin finishes in the cranberry opal color.

CHRYSANTHEMUM SWIRL
(Formerly Chrysanthemum Base Swirl)

MAKER: American Glass Co., Anderson, Ind., or possibly Buckeye Glass Co., Martin's Ferry, Oh. (both involving John F. Miller)
YOP: Circa 1888-1890
COLORS: Flint, blue & cranberry opalescent; shiny or satin; no yellow opalescent known
REPROS: None
NOTES: The unique bar bottle (which has opalescent swirls leaning in the opposite direction) and the straw holder are two shapes mentioned in Northwood displays of this 1888-1889 period, leading me to hold slight reservations these may be Northwood. It seems unlikely that Buckeye would make two so very similar patterns, indicating a copy by a competitor. Most likely candidate—American Glass Co., opened by a former Buckeye manager. REVERSE SWIRL is common in yellow opalescent— CHRYSANTHEMUM SWIRL is almost unknown in this color, indicating different manufacturers. The base of both patterns sometimes contains a waffled effect. Why the yellow opalescent is so rare is a mystery, since a toothpick is known in yellow speckled (*1000TPH, Fig. 150*). All in all, the attribution is still an educated guess.

The grouping of the Fig. 60 tankard with the pattern is based on the swirls and ribs leaning in the same direction as CHRYS-ANTHEMUM SWIRL. It is not technically the same design, which has the vertical ribbing at the base. A rare tumbler was made to match this tankard, indicating it may have been a copy by a competing firm, such as Northwood (see notes under tumblers shown here).

This straw jar has long been thought to be CHRYSANTHEMUM (BASE) SWIRL, but there are now enough differences known to conclude that this, the bar bottle and possibly other shapes are simply look-alikes. We know Northwood made a straw jar in 1889 and a bar bottle in 1890, at the time he was producing cranberry opalescent

Comparison of bases on OPAL SWIRL and CHRYSANTHEMUM SWIRL star jars. The one on the left is either Hobbs or Beaumont (most likely latter). The one on the right is either a Northwood or John F. Miller design (involving several possible factories)

Cranberry opalescent butter and sugar shaker in CHRYSANTHEMUM SWIRL, by either Buckeye or American Glass Co.

CHRYSANTHEMUM SWIRL water pitcher in cranberry

Scarce tall salt shaker in cranberry CHRYSAN-THEMUM SWIRL. The shorter size is shown as Fig. 57A & B)

REVERSE SWIRL

MAKER: Buckeye Glass Co., Martin's Ferry, Oh.
YOP: circa 1888-1890
OMN: Buckeye's No. 528 line
COLORS: white, blue, canary and cranberry opalescent; shiny or satin finish; also speckled finish
REPROS: none
NOTES: See also COLLARED REVERSE SWIRL

ITEMS KNOWN:
1. Water pitcher (55)
2. Tumblers (56)
3. Cruet (65)
4. Salt shakers (64) Other similars
5. Syrup (67)
6. Butter
7. Covered Sugar (63)
8. Creamer
9. Spooner (62)
10. Master Berry Bowl (several sizes)
11. Sauce
12. Sugar shaker (66)
13. Oil lamp (several sizes)
14. Lamp shades
15. Custard cup
16. Mustard pot
17. Toothpick holder
18. Night lamps (*Smith1, Fig. 509, p. 209*)
19. Finger bowl
20. Water bottles (2 sizes)

COLLECTOR'S NOTES:

Both the master berry bowl, and the cruet, salt/pepper, and mustard were made to fit a spiral silver plated frame. Thus we have a brides' basket and a seasoning (or castor) set. It is quite possible that the spooner is the most prevalent piece of the table set. Perhaps more spooners were made for the express purpose of creating a pickle castor.

The oil lamp is highly sought after by both lamp buffs and collectors of opalescent glass. Catherine Thuro in her first book on oil lamps (*Thuro 1*), which is the foremost published material on this subject, named this lamp "Sheldon Swirl".

Because of the varied items produced in this pattern and the variety of shapes available, coupled with the fact that no reproductions have been made of the pattern, make the REVERSE SWIRL one of the most collectable cranberry opalescent patterns on today's market.

JOURNAL QUOTES
1/5/1888 P&GR

The new opalescent set of the BUCK-EYE GLASS CO. is a daisy [a Victorian term meaning a beauty—not a flower]. *It is just out and ready for the spring trade and all the dealers who have seen it have ordered freely.* **The number is 528 and there are four** colors of it, canary, blue, crystal and ruby [REVERSE SWIRL]. *In the same goods casters* [in metal holders] *and water sets will be made. The Buckeye is getting there in good shape. It shut down on Saturday for a week or ten days to take stock and make needed repairs. Several additions are being made. The middle furnace will probably be started in the near future. Business is good.*

3/1/1888 P&GR

MARTIN'S FERRY—THE BUCKEYE is running almost entirely on its 528 opalescent pattern on which it is having a good run. Messrs. Gottschalk and Leichti are out on the road.

Two sizes in REVERSE SWIRL oil lamps by Buckeye Glass Co., Martin's Ferry, Oh.

The caster set is Buckeye, in the REVERSE SWIRL pattern, with a blue cruet, yellow mustard and cranberry shakers. The tankard pitcher next to it has swirls angling in the opposite direction, indicating it is the mystery variant of CHRYSAN-THEMUM SWIRL (Northwoods?)

The direction of the swirls indicates this is not REVERSE SWIRL, but a finger bowl in CHRYSANTHMUM SWIRL (or its similar variant)

COLLARED REVERSE SWIRL

MAKER: Model Flint Glass Works, Albany, Ind.

YOP: Circa 1901-1902

COLORS: white, blue and canary opalescent; also speckled finish; no cranberry known

REPROS: none

NOTE: The similarity to REVERSE SWIRL and CHRYSANTHEMUM SWIRL is no accident. This is the third pattern made under a patent held by John F. Miller, who managed the Albany factory, and earlier managed the Buckeye and American glass factories.

There is a slight possibility that the Fig. 60 tankard and the third tumbler shown in this section were made for this set. However, the cranberry color and the swirls leaning in the opposite direction tend to rule this out.

ITEMS KNOWN:
1. Butter
2. Creamer
3. Covered sugar
4. Spooner
5. Syrup pitcher
6. Toothpick holder (*1000TPH, Fig. 168*)

COLLARED REVERSE SWIRL syrup pitcher, a design introduced by John Miller at Albany, Ind.

Some pieces of the Buckeye and Model Flint versions of the pattern could be confusing, especially the rose bowl shown here (Model) next to a mustard pot in speckled REVERSE SWIRL (Buckeye)

Small night lamps in REVERSE SWIRL, colors unknown

Our "NOVELTY" OPALESCENT Assortment.

An Assortment with Which You Can Double Your Money or Paralyze Competition by Retailing for 10 Cents.

C863—The newest and most beautiful articles in rich opalescent colorings, all in new shades and patterns in 3 delicate colors; blue, flint and canary opalescent. Most of them could be retailed for 25 cents.

Asst. Comprises 1-2 Doz. Each of the Following:

7¼-Inch **Extra Deep Footed** Round Bowl — Rich ribbed basket pattern and fancy beaded edge.

Extra Large Footed Rose Bowl — With bent-in crimped top. A piece that always sells.

9¼-In. **Extra Large Tulip Shaped Vase** — Ribbed spiral pattern, wide base crimped top.

8-In. **Extra Large Footed Plate** or **Card Tray** — Beautiful pattern, beaded edge.

Extra Heavy Tankard Milk or **Cream Pitcher** — With stuck handle, heavy ribbed pattern, very rich.

9-In. **Extra Large Salad Dish** — With crimped edge. Cheap at 25 cents.

6-In. **Large Tall Celery Holder** — Fancy crimped edge, elaborate pattern.

7¼-In. **Fancy Footed Tray or Plate** — Brilliant ribbed pattern, beaded edge.

5¼-In. **High Footed Deep Bowl** — For jellies, etc.

7-In. **Deep Flaring Table Dish** — Artistic pattern. A beauty.

7¼x5 **Footed Fancy Shape Utility Dish** — Heavy rolled-up edges.

6¼x6¼ **Extra Large Footed Dish** — Square shape, bent-up sides.

(*Total 6 doz. in bbl., wt. 97 lbs. Bbl. 35c*)

Per dozen. 80c

This 1902 assortment of pressed and blown opalescent includes a FERN celery vase and a COLLARED REVERSE SWIRL rose bowl among

several pieces of RIBBED SPIRAL. These were products of Model Flint Glass Works, while John F. Miller was in charge

Two sizes of REVERSE SWIRL water bottles, made Buckeye Glass Company

COLLARED REVERSE SWIRL covered butter, which indicates a full table set was made. But due to the closing of the Model factory in late 1902, the production of this pattern was limited, and all pieces are quite rare. An original factory sticker found on the bottom of this butter is shown on page 28

RIBBED OPAL RINGS
(Formerly RIBBED OPAL SPIRAL)

MAKER: Probably Northwood at Martin's Ferry, O.
YOP: circa 1888
COLORS: white, blue, and cranberry opalescent
REPROS: a later version (without ribs) by Fenton in 1930's
AKA: RIBBED OPAL SPIRAL (too often confused for RIBBED SPIRAL, a popular pressed pattern)
NOTES: The name is being changed here since the opalescent rings are not connecting (or spiralling). The tumbler shown in black and white shows that each "ring" is unconnected.

Northwood came out with two lines of "fancy" glass in 1888, and since this pattern is made from the same shape molds as RIBBED COINSPOT, perhaps this was one of the two lines. There are almost no other possibilities.

ITEMS KNOWN:
1. Water pitcher (249)
2. Tumbler (243)
3. Sugar bowl

COLLECTOR'S NOTES:
The water pitcher, tumblers, and covered sugar bowl are the only pieces to surface in this pattern. The water pitcher is a unusual short tankard. The covered sugar carries the same finial as the RIBBED COINSPOT sugar. The water pitchers in both patterns are from the same mold. It would be in line to suspect that the rest of the table set (butter, spooner, and creamer) exist, but none has been documented to date. There are no reproductions on this exact pattern, only a similar "ringed" line by Fenton in 1930's.

RIBBED OPAL RINGS tumbler, which I previously called by another name. However, the opalescent rings do not connect in a spiralling fashion, and the other name could have easily been confused for a pressed pattern with a similar name

OPAL SWIRL in ROYAL OAK mold

MAKER: The Northwood Glass Company at Martin's Ferry, Ohio
YOP: circa 1891
COLORS: only cranberry opalescent reported to date
REPROS: none
NOTES: This must have been experimental. It is an important piece in that it helps confirm Northwood had OPAL SWIRL spot molds and may have made the straw holder in this pattern (a shape described in trade journals).

ITEMS KNOWN:
1. Creamer (272)

The shape mold for the ROYAL OAK creamer was used to form this rare example using an Opalescent SWIRL secondary motif. This is the only one known to date, and was undoubtedly experimental in nature

COLLECTOR'S NOTES:
Only one piece has been found to date. (See PGP1, p. 1) for photograph of their fantastic piece. It is difficult to know if this piece is experimental or part of a more extensive production. However, the ROYAL OAK pattern was made with great frequency in the rubina and frosted rubina colors. Probably few pieces exist with the secondary SWIRL pattern.

OPAL SWIRL
in NORTHWOOD JEWEL mold

MAKER: The Northwood Glass Works at Martin's Ferry, Ohio
YOP: circa 1890
COLORS: only cranberry opalescent reported to date
REPROS: none
NOTES: Another shape in SWIRL motif. It opens up many exciting possibilities on other possible shape molds for opalescent production: ROYAL IVY, LEAF MOLD, LEAF UMBRELLA

ITEMS KNOWN:
1. Salt shaker

COLLECTOR'S NOTES:
Again another limited, perhaps experimental production of using the opal swirl on the "Threaded Swirl" (OMN: Northwood's JEWEL) pattern—which usually appears in rubina glass. (See *PGP1, p. 1* for a photograph of this beautifully executed salt shaker.)

Another Northwood line which he called JEWEL was used as a shape mold for this salt shaker in OPAL SWIRL. It is blue opalescent

Presented here is more evidence that Northwood made the straw jar on the cover. The tumbler on the left is CHRYSANTHEMUM SWIRL. The one in the center is REVERSE SWIRL. The one on the right was made to accompany the Fig. 60 tankard. Note the ribs are leaning on the tankard but perpendicular on the tumbler. The ribs above the "Chrysanthemum Base" are also perpendicular on the straw jar. On all other items they lean. Compare the slightly different finial on the straw jar to the Fig. 71 covered butter.

An 1890 trade journal described a "Twist" salt and pepper which is probably the example shown here in blue opalescent at the left. In the center is a CHRYSANTHEMUM SWIRL custard cup and on the right what seems to be a second taller salt shaker in REVERSE SWIRL.

A white opalescent shot glass in REVERSE SWIRL, an unlisted shape. Also shown is a view of the base to a CHRYSANTHEMUM SWIRL cruet, which reveals a waffle-like effect found under most pieces. This design does not clearly appear on the straw jar bottom. However, it is possible, indeed likely, that these molds were made for both Northwood and Miller by Hipkins, who is known to have done work for both men. If Miller failed to purchase the straw jar mold then it may have been bought by Northwood.

UNITED STATES PATENT OFFICE.

JOHN F. MILLER, OF MARTIN'S FERRY, OHIO.

METHOD OF MANUFACTURING ORNAMENTAL GLASS.

SPECIFICATION forming part of Letters Patent No. 393,257, dated November 20, 1888.

Application filed March 10, 1888. Serial No. 266,819. (No model.)

To all whom it may concern:

Be it known that I, JOHN F. MILLER, a citizen of the United States of America, residing at Martin's Ferry, in the county of Belmont and State of Ohio, have invented certain new and useful Improvements in Method of Manufacturing Ornamental Glassware, of which the following is a specification, reference being had therein to the accompanying drawings.

My invention relates to an improved method of manufacturing ornamental glassware.

My invention consists in the method hereinafter described of manufacturing ornamental glassware, which consists in first blowing the glass bulb in a corrugated mold, so as to form ridges thereon, then reheating the same, so as to develop the ridges into an opalescent color, then twisting the bulb, so that the ridges will assume a spiral form thereon, and, finally, blowing the article in a ribbed or fluted mold to form grooves and ridges crossing the opalescent spirals in the article.

For the purpose of better illustrating my invention, I have shown in Figure 1 a vertical sectional view of a mold in which the glass is first blown to form ridges thereon. Fig. 2 is a top or plan view of the mold shown in Fig. 1. Fig. 3 is a vertical sectional view of the mold in which the article is finished. Fig. 4 is a top or plan view of the mold shown in Fig. 3. Fig. 5 is a view in perspective of the punty or blow-pipe with the glass bulb thereon after it has been blown in the mold shown in Figs. 1 and 2. Fig. 6 is a view in perspective of the punty or blow-pipe with the glass thereon, showing the operation of forming the spirals thereon. Fig. 7 is a side view of the blow-pipe with the glass thereon, showing the spiral ribs after the twisting or twirling process has been performed.

A indicates a mold having longitudinal ribs or flutes B for forming ribs or ridges on the article in the first step of the process.

C indicates a mold in which the article is finished, and is also provided with longitudinal flutes or corrugations for decorating the outside of the article with flutes or corrugations.

In carrying out my invention, the "blower" gathers on his blow-pipe the proper amount of glass, and after rolling the same on a marver, to bring it to a round and oblong shape, he places it in the mold A, and blows sufficiently hard to cause the hot glass to take the same shape as the inside of the mold A, and as shown in Fig. 5. The corrugated glass bulb is now reheated in the "glory hole," and the ribs or corrugations, which have become partially cold, are, upon being reheated, turned white, while the main body of the glass, which has not become cooled, retains its original color. After the bulb has been reheated, as above stated, the blower places the lower end of the bulb on the marver, and turns or twirls the blow pipe, so as to twist the glass and cause the white ribs or flutes to assume a spiral form around the bulb. The bulb is now placed in the mold shown in Figs. 3 and 4, and blown to form longitudinal ribs and grooves, which cross the spiral lines or ribs, thus giving to the article an ornamental and finished appearance.

Articles may be made of a batch of any desired color, and while the spiral ribs may not be a pure white, as would be the case if an opalescent batch were used, yet the spiral ribs will be whiter than the intervening spaces, and whiter than the main body of the glass, which is due to the reheating of the bulb on which the initial ribs have been formed.

What I claim, and desire to secure by Letters Patent, is—

The method herein described of manufacturing ornamental glassware, which consists in first blowing the glass bulb in a corrugated mold to form ridges thereon, then reheating the bulb thus formed to develop the ridges into a whiter color than the main body of the article, then twisting or twirling the bulb, so that the ridges will assume a spiral form, and finally blowing the article in a ribbed or fluted mold to form ridges crossing the spiral stripes, as set forth.

In testimony whereof I have affixed my signature in presence of two witnesses.

JOHN F. MILLER.

Witnesses:
CHAS. S. MILLER,
G. A. McKIM.

Reprinted here is the original patent drawings and specifications for the process used in making some of the OPALESCENT SWIRL patterns shown in this section. It was patented by John F. Miller, the patent being granted in November, 1888. REVERSE SWIRL was introduced at the beginning of 1888. Other firms could have used the process in the meantime. His patent would have expired in 1905. This patent would cover the process used on REVERSE SWIRL, CHRYSANTHEMUM SWIRL, MELON RIB SWIRL, and the similar variant of CHRYSANTHEMUM SWIRL. Trade journals announce that Northwood offered a straw jar in July, 1888, which was before the Miller patent was granted. Perhaps Miller had a line of molds for tableware made by Hipkins Novelty Mold to match the basic idea of this straw jar (and similar bar bottle) when he was ordering molds for his own short-lived American Glass Co., at Anderson, Ind.

(No Model.)   2 Sheets—Sheet 1.

J. F. MILLER.
METHOD OF MANUFACTURING ORNAMENTAL GLASS.

No. 393,257.   Patented Nov. 20, 1888.

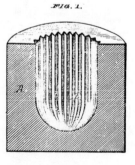

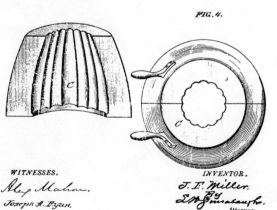

WITNESSES,
Alex Mahon.
Joseph A. Ryan.

INVENTOR.
J. F. Miller.
BY
S. M. Zinsabaugh,
Attorney.

(No Model.)   2 Sheets—Sheet 2.

J. F. MILLER.
METHOD OF MANUFACTURING ORNAMENTAL GLASS.

No. 393,257.   Patented Nov. 20, 1888.

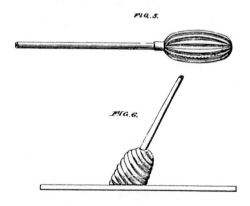

WITNESSES,
Alex Mahon.
Joseph A. Ryan.

INVENTOR.
J. F. Miller.
BY
S. M. Zinsabaugh,
Attorney.

Miscellaneous Patterns

BLOWN HOBNAIL

MAKERS: Hobbs, Brockunier & Co., continued by Hobbs Glass Co., and U.S. Glass (Factory H); copied by Northwood at La Belle Glass Co., Bridgeport, O. in a variety of shapes; also some shapes made by Beaumont and Northwood at their own factories
YOP: Introduced in 1886—still made in 1900
COLORS: white, blue, yellow, rubina and cranberry opalescent; also in cased glass colors
REPROS: similar shapes made in Czechoslovakia; barber bottle reproduced by L.G. Wright (made at Fenton factory) in late 1930's.
NOTES: Long thought to be exclusive to Hobbs, Brockunier, it now appears that LaBelle also made a similar line of BLOWN HOBNAIL in cranberry opalescent and cased colors. A January, 1887, trade journal noted the line was "novel". The Hobbs line was introduced in 1886. The cased colors in pink, white, mauve, etc. seem to be LaBelle. Also made at Phoenix, called "Wart".

SHAPES KNOWN:
1. Water pitchers of varying sizes (167)
2. Tumblers (171)
3. Cruet (168)
4. Syrup (253)
5. Butter (376—pressed lid is white)
6. Covered Sugar
7. Creamer
8. Spooner
9. Barber bottles (166, 303-305)
10. Master Berry bowl (170)
11. Sauce (169)
12. Water bottle
13. Finger bowl—underplate
14. Celery vase
15. Lamp shades
16. Oval relish bowl
17. Crimp top vase (213)
18. Quart pitcher (377)

COLLECTOR'S NOTES:
From 1930 to 1939 a Czechoslovakian reproduction was imported for the American market. Many shapes and sizes were produced. To add further confusion to the collecting of hobnail, both the Duncan Miller and Fenton Art Glass factories made

Hobnail in the 40's. All three companies made shapes that were never originally produced by Hobbs, Brockunier in the 1880's.

The Imperial Glass Co. of Bellaire, OH, is another factory which re-made the opalescent Hobnail pattern. According to Dorothy Hammond in her *Confusing Collectibles* (pages 58 and 59), this pressed version was made in vaseline opalescent. There is no indication that Imperial ran a production of cranberry. However, it is startling to see pictured among the Imperial reproduction the old Hobbs covered sugar bowl (on page 59—listed as jar and cover). This sugar bowl does not have a fire polished pontil—which is a good guide when searching for old Hobbs Hobnail.

Always remember when judging a piece of opalescent hobnail, that the original was

hand made by a proud and quality-controlled factory—in a place when artisans worked for little money—in a completely different time than the mechanization of the machine age which was to follow. Inspect the base of a hobnail piece—the old Hobbs Brockunier HOBNAIL of the 1880's always incorporated the fire polished pontil in the finished product.

The Czechoslovakians did blow their production of hobnail—all of the pieces have a pontil scar which was never subjected to the workmans polishing wheel when the piece was finished.

Some old pieces have reeded handles. This is primarily found on water pitchers. However, the polished pontil should take prescidence over the reeding in the handle. Even the Czechoslovakian production uses plain and reeded handles. The Fenton pro-

Assortment of Hobbs, Brockunier & Co.'s No. 333 BLOWN HOBNAIL, from circa 1888 catalogue

duction used reeded and "pinched" handle techniques in their production.

The opalescent Hobnail cruet reproduction has provided the collector with still another area of confusion. Both old and new have plain (not reeded) handles. In the Hammond *Confusing Collectibles* (page 61), the author shows a Rubina Verde Opal reproduction Cruet. Even author Dean L. Murray in his second book *More Cruets Only* was duped by this good reproduction. Because Mr. Murray photographed Czechoslovakian, reproduction, and old Hobbs Hobnail cruets together (page 48-49), it is best to study the photograph in the *More Cruets Only* book: top row—Cruet #1, 2, 3 are Czechoslovakian cruets. Notice each have tri-cornered spouts and the short reeded handle. These cruets have a rough pontil scar on the bottom. Cruet #4 is a recent reproduction. It has the flared tri-cornered spout and the long neck. Notice where the handle starts—high above the top row of hobs.

Middle row—Cruets #1, 2, 3, 4 are all old Hobbs Hobnail cruets. All have tri-cornered spouts, long necks, and the handle starts with (or even includes) the top row of hobs. All of these cruets have fire polished pontils.

Given this information, can you pick out the one reproduction cruet in the bottom row? (Cruets #1, 3, 4 are old).

Items never made: salt shakers, toothpick could possibly exist—none has surfaced in cranberry opal to date. However, other opal colors are known to exist in the old Hobbs molds.

JOURNAL QUOTES:
8/26/1886 P&GR

Hobbs, Brockunier & Co., of Wheeling, have out a new set, No.102, [SUNBURST AND BAR—H6, p. 61] which is an imitation of cut glass. They make it in all colors, also in crystal and decorated in amber. This is very beautiful ware and difficult to tell from cut. Their No.323 [HOBNAIL] opalescent pressed ware is very attractive and they claim a patent on it. They have also out a new line of fancy finger bowls and fruit bowls, as well as a new line of fancy globes and shades.

1/27/1887 P&GR

The La Belle Co.'s new line of opalescent tableware, the "Dew-drop", is simply superb, and those wanting something rich and novel for the spring trade should lose no time in ordering it. This firm have made a marked success in the production of fine colored glass and their latest effort is worthy of their previous successes.

3/17/1887 P&GR

The La Belle has just started its second furnace and has about all it can do to fill orders for their new line of plain and opalescent table ware, new line of rock crystal, new effects and shapes in globes. The ware made here is hard to beat. A visit to their

sample room is a pleasure. It is well filled with artistic novelties in tableware, bar ware, lamps, stationers' gas and kerosene goods, canary, amber, blue, topaz, rose de Barry, ruby, citron, pomona, ivory, turquoise, allochrite and all opalescent colors. The outlook is very good.

This yellow cased glass pitcher clearly appears to be a Hobbs shape, but is it. La Belle Glass also made a line they called "Dew-drop" and were capable of making many cased glass colors in which BLOWN HOBNAIL is known. There are at least two different molds known on the small berry dish and also on the celery vase. The pitchers come in varying sizes by Hobbs, but some examples with reeded handles may be La Belle.

Yellow opalescent HOBNAIL cruet with reeded handle. Is this La Belle or more likely a Czechoslovakian example?

Water bottle in cranberry BLOWN HOBNAIL, probably Hobbs, Brockunier

BLOWN OPAL DRAPERY

MAKERS: National Glass Co., operating Northwood Glass Works, Indiana, Pa.
YOP: Advertised in 1903
AKA: Northwood BLOWN DRAPES
COLORS: white, blue, canary, green and cranberry opalescent
SHAPE MOLDS: NINE PANEL sugar shaker
REPROS: limited L.G. Wright cruets
NOTES: Similar pattern was made by Fenton in a water set with a pressed tumbler—no cranberry known.

ITEMS KNOWN:
1. Water pitcher (172) others
2. Tumblers (173)
3. Barber bottle
4. Cruet (184—probably Wright)

COLLECTOR'S NOTES:
While a cruet does exist in this pattern, because of the ruffled top, reeded handle, and weight, it is highly doubtful that it is an old piece of glass. I know of no old American pattern glass cruet (excluding art glass) which use a ruffled top! Its collectibility does not lie in its age, but rather in its scarcity; it does not lie in the fact that it is Northwood (which it probably isn't), but rather in its uniqueness. I highly suspect this cruet was made by L. G. Wright in the 1940's or 50's.

Rare Cranberry BLOWN OPAL DRAPERY barber bottle.

BLOWN TWIST

MAKERS: National Glass Co., operating Northwood Glass Works, Indiana, Pa.
YOP: advertised in 1903
COLORS: white, blue, canary, green and cranberry opalescent
SHAPE MOLDS: NINE PANEL sugar shaker
REPROS: SWIRLED FEATHER line by Fenton in 1950's and recent years
NOTES: The spot mold used on BLOWN OPAL DRAPERY is the same one used on BLOWN TWIST, with the pattern angled or "twisted" dramatically.

SHAPES KNOWN:
1. Water pitcher (175)
2. Tumblers (176)
3. Sugar shaker (205)

COLLECTOR'S NOTES:
A very limited cranberry opalescent pattern. The most attractive piece of which must be considered the water pitcher. Both the unusual shape and twisted (not reeded) opalescent handle find this pitcher a unique beauty.

the Fenton Art Glass Company produced a pattern called Swirled Feather in the 1950's which resemble the BLOWN TWIST pattern. However, none of the three original items (water pitcher, tumbler, or sugar shaker) were mady by Fenton. I do not consider the SWIRLED FEATHER a reproduction of the OPAL TWIST line. Therefore, I feel that this pattern has never been reproduced.

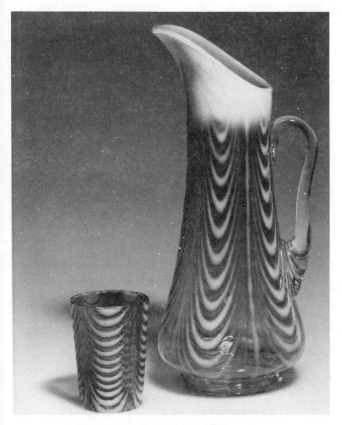

Cranberry BLOWN OPAL DRAPERY tumbler and tankard, made by the Northwood Glass Works of National Glass Co., at Indiana, Pa., circa 1903

A 1903 Butler Bros. pictured a BLOWN OPAL DRAPERY and BLOWN TWIST water set assortment. These were made by the Northwood Glass Works of the National Glass Co., but Harry Northwood was no longer involved in the factories activities at the time

CHRISTMAS SNOWFLAKE

MAKER: Northwood, location uncertain
YOP: Circa 1888-1898
COLORS: white, blue and cranberry opalescent
SHAPE MOLD: Water pitcher same as found on a variant of LATTICE
REPROS: See L.G. Wright reprints
RESEARCH NOTES: This "snowflake" is more flower than flake. Compare Fig. 183 to Fig. 95, a Northwood mold. The oil lamps and night lamps, known as SNOWFLAKE, are in a variant which lacks the lattice design at the base.

ITEMS KNOWN:
1. Water Pitcher (178, 183—Ribbed and Plain)
2. Tumblers (179, 182)
3. Cruet (N. Swirl mold—only white reported to date)
4. Vase? (unconfirmed, but a woodcutting is shown on old Northwood letterhead from Ellwood City.)

COLLECTOR'S NOTES:
The water pitcher comes in two different shapes. The same is true with the tumble—there is a ribbed and a plain mold. Only one cruet has emerged in this pattern and it was in the NORTHWOOD SWIRL Mold (see H6, p. 11). This is a case where there are more reproduction pieces than old ones.

In 1980 L.G. Wright re-issued the pattern in the plain (non-ribbed or swirled) variety. More new pieces were made than old: water pitchers, tumblers, creamer, barber bottles, sugar shaker, small basket, small rose bowl, large rose bowl, milk pitchers, syrup, oval cruet, and wedding (as brides) bowl. The cost of the new water pitcher was $160.

White opalescent CHRISTMAS SNOWFLAKE cruet blown into same shape mold used on Northwood's PARIAN SWIRL and DAISY AND FERN cruets

This "Cottage" sewing lamp is better known as the SNOWFLAKE lamp, appearing in a Christmas, 1892, Butler Bros. catalogue

SNOWFLAKE LAMPS

MAKER: Hobbs & U.S. Glass
YOP: 1891-93
COLORS: white, blue and cranberry opalescent
REF: *Smith 1,* Figs. 473-474
1892-93 *BB*
REPROS: None
NOTES: The floral design is quite different from CHRISTMAS SNOWFLAKE. This pattern lacks the lattice design along the bottom and the "flowers" are actually stars

ITEMS KNOWN:
1. Oil lamps (180, 181)
1. Hand lamp (*Smith1,* p. 51, Fig. 40)
2. Night lamp (186)

JOURNAL QUOTE:

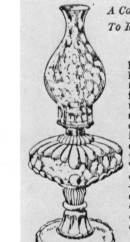

"COTTAGE" Sewing Lamp.
A Completely Fitted Lamp
To Run at a Quick-Moving Price

This beautiful opalescent lamp, standing 17½ inches high, has globe chimney of the same pattern and material as the body which is fitted to the base by a patent screw sleeve (which greatly lessens the danger of breakage in packing). The lamp is complete with burner and wick, all ready for the oil. The assortment includes 4 each of the following colors—Ruby opalescent, pearl opalescent and turquoise opalescent. Total of 1 doz. complete lamps to bbl. (Sold only by bbl.)
Price, $6.40 Doz.
......Order here.

5/14/1891 C&GJ
The Hobbs Glass Co. report trade moderate, but mail orders are coming in better now than they have been for some time past. This company have ooout an elegant new ice cream tray and saucers, made in crystal, plain or with gold finished edge, and they have made a great hit on a new line of lamps just ready for the trade. It is a square-shaped bowl made in crystal and three colors, viz.; blue opalescent, ruby opalescent and white opalescent. Its superior advantages promise a great sale for it. The bowl and foot of these lamps are screwed firmly together by a metal socket, which entirely obviates the excessive breakage attending all blown lamps. The socket is covered by a glass sleeve which conceals the metal, producing a brilliant effect and making practically an all glass lamp. The saving in breakage will make a handsome profit for the dealer. The lamps will be shown in the JOURNAL next week.

ENAMELED DECORATED BLOWN WATER SET ASSORTMENT.

A new and rich dollar leader.

C668—Comprising 3 styles, one a tall fancy fluted shape jug with hand painted enamel decorations in a beautiful delicate vine pattern, and one a tall wide flare top jug with elaborate floral and leaf decorations; the other an extra large swell shape jug with fancy crimped edge, with rich decorations and a wide etched band and floral enameled design. Each set consisting of one jug and 6 tumblers decorated to match, all the decorations being burnt in. The three styles being equally assorted in 3 colors, namely, green, blue and amethyst. (Total 9 sets in bbl. Bbl 85c.) Per set. 65c

This May, 1903 Butler Bros. assortment of decorated pitchers shows that the shape mold used by Northwood on his plain CHRISTMAS SNOWFLAKE pitcher (without ribs) was also used on other types of ware

Our "OPALESCENT" Lamp Assortment.
Three Popular Priced Sellers.

These lamps are of different sizes and shapes but are in the same rich opalescent dot pattern, being assorted equally in ruby opalescent, crystal opalescent and torquoise opalescent. The standard lamps are fitted with the patent screw sleeve and all are arranged for No. 1 burners.

1½ doz. Asst. Hand Lamps at $1.20, $1.80			
1 " Hand or Stand Lamps			1.88
1 " Stand or Table Lamps			1.79

Total for package........ $5.47

..... Order here.

1892 Butler Bros. assortment of SNOWFLAKE hand, stand and table lamps, offered in "ruby opalescent, crystal opalescent, and turquoise opalescent." These were made by U.S. Glass Co. at their factory H (formerly Hobbs Glass Co.) at Wheeling, W.Va.

OPAL STARS & STRIPES

MAKERS: Probably designed by Percy Beaumont for Hobbs Glass Co., with molds later used (or copied) at Beaumont Glass Co.

YOP: circa 1890; reintroduced in 1899

COLORS: white, blue and cranberry opalescent

REPROS: L.G. Wright, made by Fenton

NOTES: There is some controversy about the OPAL STARS AND STRIPES water pitcher. It was reportedly made by L.G. Wright to go with the many tumblers on the market. But no water pitcher appears in any of the catalogues from this firm. Pitchers with and without polished pontil scars are known, the latter "assumed" by many to be the Wright reproduction. But I have a theory that the version without the pontil scar is the later Beaumont production of the pattern. Both versions of this pitcher, shaped identically, are very rare. If Wright did indeed have a second larger spot mold made for a water pitcher (a smaller spot mold was used on all tumblers, creamers, cruets and barber bottles), why was such a popular pattern discontinued? The POLKA DOT pitcher with clover-leaf top is known with or without a polished pontil scar. The latter on these were also believed to be reproductions. In my opinion, they are not.

ITEMS KNOWN:
1. Water pitcher (163)
2. Tumblers
3. Barber Bottle (164, 307-308)
4. Lamp shades
5. Finger bowl
6. Cruet (165)

COLLECTOR'S NOTES:

Such a beautiful and attractive opalescent pattern. Such a hard to find opalescent pattern. Such a limited amount of items made in an opalescent pattern. And such a highly reproduced opalescent pattern. Let's see if we can sort it out: The water pitcher must have a polished pontil in order to be old! The same is true with the barber bottle! (see another opinion above)

The tumbler, which has been highly reproduced, is one of the hardest items to determine age. The tumbler and finger bowl were polished at the top. As a result, they do

not have polished pontils in the base. Usually the reproductions are heavier in weight. The old tumbler will have a "molded ledge" around the base — the reproductions have no "sitting ledge".

I have never see a lamp shade other than in a catalog reprint. I am certain it has never been remade. It could appear in either a 4-inch or 5-inch base. It would certainly be one of the rarest pieces to find in OPAL STARS AND STRIPES.

Two different style cruets have been found in this pattern. It is possible that a cruet was part of the original prodcution, although none are pictured in the original catalog reprints. Both cruets have the same shape — more oval than round, which has been a favorite of the L. G. Wright reproductions — one with plain tri-cornered top, the other with a ruffled top.

Again I must state that I know of no American pattern glass cruet (excluding the art glass production) which was ever made with a ruffled top! However, I have not ever found an advertisement for the re-issue of this cruet. I highly suspect that both cruets are of recent origin — probably 1940's or 50's. However, because of their extreme rarity, I do encourage collectors to place thme in their collections.

If ever an old STARS AND STRIPES cruet would surface, I am certain that it will have a fire polished (or possibly a rough) pontil scar on the base.

There is also a creamer (Fig. 300), with and without handle, that was never originally made. Despite the reproductions, the American theme of STARS AND STRIPES demands the respect of serious collectors.

JOURNAL QUOTE:
9/7/1899 C&GJ

*Alex P. Menzies, the New York representative of the Beaumont Glass Co., has full lines of that company's ware and is showing their latest creation for the first time this week. **It is a line of jugs in opalescent white, red and blue, with a field of stars at the bottom and stripes running up the jug.** The shapes are excellent. He has also just opened a line of crystal, sapphire and canary opalescent with gold decorations that are new and pretty* [FLORA].

Cranberry opalescent STARS AND STRIPES water pitcher, made by Hobbs and Beaumont Glass Co. It is reportedly reprduced by L.G. Wright, but these examples would be as rare as the old examples, and none appear in any known Wright catalogues

OPAL STARS AND STRIPES barber bottle, made by both Hobbs and Beaumont. It has been massively reproduced by Wright, without a polished pontil scar on the bottom. Old examples without these pontil marks may be old as well, probably the later Beaumont version

SWIRLING MAZE

MFR: The salad bowls were made by Jefferson, but it is unknown if all three known water pitchers were also made there.
YOP: circa 1901-1907
COLORS: white, blue, canary, green and cranberry opalescent
AKA: SWIRLING MAIZE (misspelled)
REPROS: none
RESEARCH NOTES: This pattern appeared in 1903 Butler Bros. catalogues in a water pitcher shape not known. (See Fig. 157.) The crimped salad bowl, which appears in the Jefferson advertisement reprinted in our history, is sometimes found with an edge treatment in speckled cranberry (which was previously thought to be a Northwood technique—now proven wrong).

SHAPEs KNOWN:
1. Water pitcher (161, 162—third shape in BB catalogue)
2. Tumblers (244)
3. Ruffled bowls (salads)

COLLECTOR'S NOTES:
   Only three items have ever been verified in this unusual and unique pattern. This pattern remains free from reproductions.

DOUBLE GREEK KEY

MAKER: Nickel-Plate Glass Co., Fostoria, Ohio, probably continued by U.S. Glass in some form after 1891
YOP: Circa 1890-92

Very rare syrup pitcher in blue opalescent DOUBLE GREEK KEY.

COLORS: white and blue opalescent
REPROS: none
RESEARCH NOTE: The blown items to this pattern are limited to the syrup pitcher, salt shaker, toothpick and mustard pot. All other items to this set are pressed.

OPAL ELLIPSE AND DIAMOND

MAKER: Unknown, but shape resembles Hobbs, Brockunier
YOP: Circa 1885-90
COLORS: Only this cranberry pitcher reported to date; blue and white likely
REPROS: None
RESEARCH NOTE: This pattern is similar to OPAL HONEYCOMB and OPAL LATTICE, but has alternating series of ellipses and diamonds, making it unique

Cranberry Opalescent

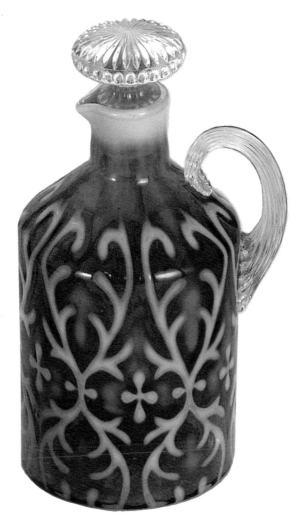

1
SPANISH LACE
(Wine Decanter)

In Color

ON THE COVER

FIGURE A—A cracker jar in SPANISH LACE, which was originally called OPALINE BROCADE by its manufacturer, The Northwood Company at Indiana, Pa. FIGURE B—OPAL HERRINGBONE water pitcher, probably made by Phoenix Glass Co., Monaca, Pa., while Harry Northwood was working there FIGURES C and D—OPAL SWIRL shot glass and champagne tumbler, probably made by Hobbs Glass Co., Wheeling, W. Va., but many other firms made this pattern FIGURE E—SWIRLED FEATHER hurricane lamp, by Fenton Art Glass Company, Williamstown, W. Va., circa 1953-1954 FIGURE F—This seems to be the CHRYS-ANTHEMUM SWIRL pattern, in a rare soda straw jar, whose manufacturer is still under investigation. This jar may be a copy by Northwood Glass Co., Martin's Ferry, Oh., but there is evidence that the rest of the line was produced by the short-lived and little-known American Glass Co., at Anderson, Ind.

Spanish Lace

5
NINE-PANEL MOLD
(Tankard)

2
RIBBON TIE MOLD
(Tankard)

3
(Tumbler)

4
SQUAT MOLD
(Pitcher)

3
(Tumbler)

10
(Cracker Jar)

6
(Butter)

7
(Spooner)

8
(Sugar)

9
(Creamer)

82

11
RIBBON TIE MOLD
(Salt & Pepper)

12
WIDE WAIST MOLD
(Sugar Shaker)

13
BALL-SHAPE MOLD
(Syrup)

14
OVAL INDIANA MOLD
(Cruet)

Daisy and Fern
(Except Fig. 19)

15
NORTHWOOD SWIRL
(Pitcher)

16A
N. SWIRL
(Tumbler)

17
BALL SHAPE
(Pitcher)

16B
(Tumbler)

18
SHOULDER MOLD
(Pitcher)

19
AISY IN CRISS-CROSS
(Bulbous Syrup)

20
N. SWIRL
(sauce)

21
N. SWIRL
(Berry Bowl)

22
N. SWIRL
(Sugar Shaker)

23
N. SWIRL
(Cruet)

24
WIDE WAIST
(Sugar Shaker)

25
(Rose Bowl)

26
APPLE BLOSSOM MOLD
(Spooner-Caster Insert)

83

Opalescent Seaweed

27
TRIANGULAR CRIMP
(Water Pitcher)

28
(Celery Vase)

29
SQUARE
(Bitters Bottle)

30
ROUND
(Bitters Bottle)

31
SQUARE-TOP
(Water Pitcher)

32
(Sugar)

33
(Butter)

34
(Spooner)

35
(Creamer)

36
BULBOUS BASE
(Toothpick)

37
BULBOUS BA
(Salt & Pepper)

84

38
BULBOUS BASE
(Cruet)

39
BULBOUS BASE
(Sugar Shaker)

40
BULBOUS BASE
(Syrup)

41
(Tumbler)

42
BULBOUS BASE
(Satin Cruet)

Consolidated Criss-Cross

43
FROSTED SATIN
(Pitcher)

44
(Salt Shaker)

45
(Toothpick)

46
(Tumbler)

47
SHINY
(Pitcher)

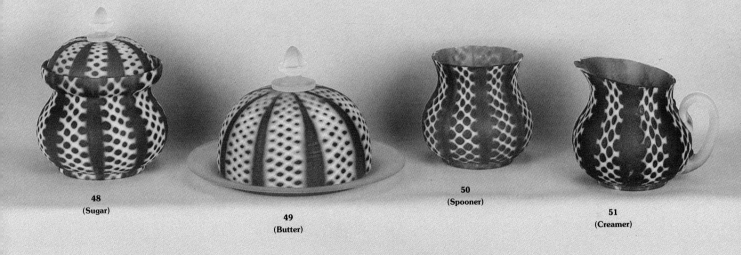

48
(Sugar)

49
(Butter)

50
(Spooner)

51
(Creamer)

52
(Satin Cruet)

53
(Shiny Butter)

54
(Shiny Cruet)

Reverse Swirl & Chrysanthemum Swirl

(R.S.)　　　　　　　　　　　　　(C.S.)

55
(R.S. Pitcher)

56
(R.S. Tumbler)

57A
(C.S. Pepper)

58
(C.S. Pitcher)

57B
(C.S. Salt)

59
(C.S. Tumbler)

60
**CHRYSANTHEMUM
SWIRL VARIANT**
(Tankard)

61
(R.S. Celery)

62
(R.S. Spooner)

63
(R.S. Sugar)

64
(R.S. Salt-Pepper)

65
(R.S. Cruet)

66
(R.S. Sugar Shaker)

67
(R.S. Syrup)

68
(C.S. Cruet)

69
(C.S. Toothpick)

70
(C.S. Spooner)

71
(C.S. Butter)

72
(C.S. Creamer)

73
(Sugar Shaker)

74
(C.S. Syrup)

Opalescent Stripe & Swirl

75
RING NECK STRIPE
(Pitcher)

76
SWIRL
(Tumbler)

77
BEAUMONT SWIRL
(Pitcher)

78
HOBBS SWIRL
(Cruet)

79
SQUARE-TOP
(Pitcher)

80
HOBBS SWIRL
(Celery Vase)

81
HOBBS SWIRL
(Sugar Shaker)

82
NICKEL SWIRL
(Sugar Shaker)

83
NICKEL SWIRL
(Cruet)

84
NICKEL SWIRL
(Toothpick)

85
HOBBS SWIRL
(Syrup Pitcher)

86
SWIRL
(Sugar Shaker)

87
STRIPE
(Shank-Shoulder Cruet)

88
STRIPE
(Shank-Waist Cruet)

89
RINK NECK STRIPE
(Cruet)

90
RING NECK STRIPE
(Toothpick)

91
STRIPE
(Barber Bottle)

Opalescent Lattice

92
BUCKEYE LATTICE
(Satin Pitcher)

93
RIBBED OPAL LATTICE
(Tankard)

94
OPAL LATTICE
(Star-crimp Pitcher)

95
OPAL LATTICE
(Twist-handle Pitcher)

96
R.O. LATTICE
(Cruet)

97
BUCKEYE LATTICE
(Satin Cruet)

98
R.O. LATTICE
(Sugar Shaker)

99
R.O. LATTICE
(Butter)

100
BUCKEYE LATTICE
(Sugar Shaker)

101
OPAL LATTICE
(Ball-base Cruet)

102
OPAL LATTICE
(Indiana Mold)

103
BUCKEYE LA
(Toothpick

104
R.O. LATTICE
(Celery)

105
R.O. LATTICE
(Tumbler)

106
R.O. LATTICE
(Salt-Pepper)

107
R.O. LATTICE
(Toothpick)

108
QUILTED PHLOX MOLD
(Salt-Pepper)

109
OPAL LATTICE
(Tumbler)

110
RIBBED PILLAR M
(Spooner-Caster Inse

Opalescent Windows

(Plain & Swirled)

111
SQUARE-TOP
(Pitcher)

112
(Tumbler)

113
WINDOWS SWIRL
(Pitcher)

114
(Tumbler)

115
TRI-CORNER CRIMP
(Pitcher)

116
(Butter)

117
(Spooner)

118
(Sugar)

119
(Creamer)

120
(Celery)

121
(Barber Bottle)

122
(Cruet)

123
(Syrup)

124
(Toothpick)

125
(Salt-Pepper)

126
(Sugar Shaker)

127
STAR-CRIMP CRIMP
(Northwood Pitcher)

128
INDIANA MOLD
(Cruet)

129
THREE-TIER TANKARD
(Northwood Pitcher)

130
(Tumbler)

131
SQUARE-TOP
(Beaumont Pitcher)

132
BALL-SHAPE
(Pitcher)

133
COINSPOT & SWIRL
(Northwood Cruet)

134
(Barber Bottle)

135
RIBBED COINSPOT
(Syrup)

136
RIBBED COINSPOT
(Pitcher)

137
RING NECK
(Cruet)

138
RING NECK
(Sugar Shaker)

139
NINE-PANEL
(Sugar Shaker)

140
WIDE WAIST
(Sugar Shaker)

141
BUCKEYE JUG
(Cruet)

142
PHOENIX JUG
(Cruet)

Fern, Polka Dot & Big Windows

143
POLKA DOT
(W. Va. Pitcher)

144
OPAL FERN
(W. Va. Pitcher)

145
SQUARE-TOP FERN
(Beaumont Pitcher)

146
BIG WINDOWS
(Buckeye Pitcher)

147
OPAL. FERN
(Barber Bottle)

148
OPAL FERN
(Syrup)

149
OPAL FERN
(Sugar Shaker)

150
OPAL FERN
(W.Va. Optic Mold)

151
OPAL FERN
(Cruet)

152
OPAL FERN
(Tumbler)

153
OPAL HONEYCOMB
(Decor. Tumbler)

154
POLKA DOT
(W. Va. Syrup)

155
POLKA DOT
(Indiana Mold Cruet)

156
POLKA DOT
(Indiana Mold Syrup)

Miscellaneous Opalescent

157
BUTTONS AND BRAIDS
(Pitcher)

158
(Tumbler)

159
ARABIAN NIGHTS
(Pitcher)

160
(Tumbler)

161
SWIRLING MAZE
(Shoulder-Shape)

162
SWIRLING MAZE
(Pitcher)

163
STARS & STRIPES
(Pitcher)

164
STARS & STRIPES
(Barber Bottle)

165
STARS & STRIPES
(Indiana Mold)

166
HOBNAIL
(Barber Bottle)

167
HOBNAIL
(Pitcher)

168
HOBNAIL
(Cruet)

169
HOBNAIL
(Sauce)

170
HOBNAIL
(Berry Bowl)

171
HOBNAIL
(Tumbler)

Miscellaneous Opalescent

172
LOWN OPAL DRAPERY
(Tankard)

173
(Tumbler)

174
POINSETTIA
(Pitcher)

175
BLOWN TWIST
(Pitcher)

176
(Tumbler)

177
POINSETTIA
(Tankard)

178
CHRISTMAS SNOWFLAKE
(Ribbed Pitcher)

179
(Tumbler)

180
SNOWFLAKE
(Oil Lamp)

181
SNOWFLAKE
(Oil Lamp)

182
(No. 2 Tumbler)

183
CHRISTMAS SNOWFLAKE
(Twist-handle Pitcher)

184
BLOWN OPAL DRAPERY
(Indiana Mold Cruet)

185
POINSETTIA
(Fruit Bowl)

186
SNOWFLAKE
(Night Lamp)

93

Miscellaneous Opalescent

187
OPAL STRIPE
(Caster Set)

188
OPAL SEAWEED
(Pickle Caster)

189
OPAL SWIRL
(Hall Shade)

190
NORTHWOOD SWIRL
(Bar Bottle)

191
REVERSE SWIRL
(Oil Lamp)

192
DAISY & FERN
(N. Swirl Syrup)

193
COINSPOT
(Indiana Mold)

194
COINSPOT
(Sugar Shaker)

195
COINSPOT
(Hobbs' Syrup)

196
RIBBED COINSPOT
(Sugar Shaker)

197
OPAL LATTICE
(Buckeye Syrup)

198
SWASTIKA
(Indiana Mold)

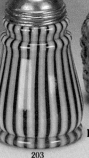

200
CONSOLIDATED
CRISS-CROSS

202
POLKA DOT
(W. Va. Mold)

204
DAISY & FERN
(N. Swirl Mold)

206
WIDE STRIPE
(Nickel Mold)

199
OPAL DIAMONDS
(Coloratura Mold)

201
POLKA DOT
(Fancy Fans Mold)

203
OPAL STRIPE
(Buckeye?)

205
BLOWN TWIST
(Nine Panel Mold)

207
OPAL SWI
(Hobbs Mold)

Miscellaneous Opalescent

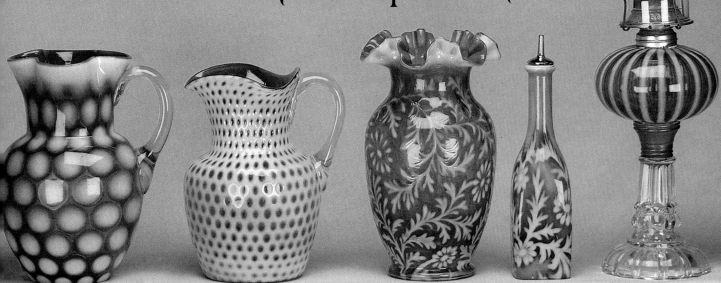

208
COINSPOT
(W. Va. Mold)

209
OPAL WINDOWS
(Tri-Corner Mouth)

210
DAISY & FERN
(Vase)

211
DAISY & FERN
(Square Barber Bottle)

212
OPAL STRIPE
(Oil Lamp)

213
HOBNAIL
(Vase)

214
BIG WINDOWS
(Butter)

215
BIG WINDOWS
(Creamer)

216
OPAL SWIRL
(Cruet)

217
LADY OPAL
(Toothpick)

218
OPAL STRIPE
(Jack-in-the-Pulpit)

221
FLORAL EYELET
(Tumbler)

222-223
OPALESCENT FERN
(Sauce and Berry Bowl)

219-220
CHRYSANTHEMUM SWIRL
(Sauce and Berry Bowl)

Miscellaneous Opalescent

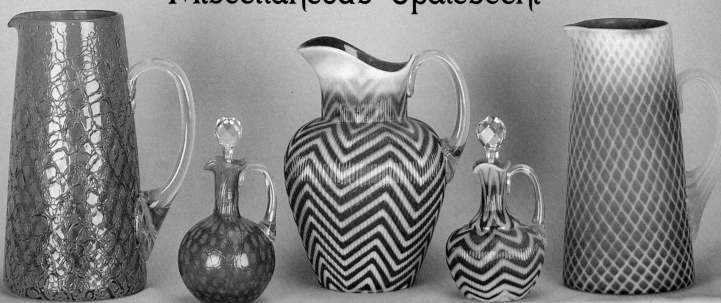

224
OPALESCENT DIAMONDS
(Crackled Tankard)

225
OPALESCENT DIAMONDS
(Crackled Cruet)

226-227
OPAL HERRINGBONE
(Pitcher)   (Cruet)

228
OPALESCENT LATTICE
(Satin Tankard)

229
OPALESCENT ELLIPSE & DIAMOND
(Squat Ball Pitcher)

230
WIDE STRIPE
(Pitcher)

231
OPALESCENT HONEYCOMB
(Square Top Pitcher)

232
OPAL HERRINGBONE
(Tumbler)

233
VINEYARD
(Decanter)

Miscellaneous Opalescent

234
OPALESCENT DIAMONDS
(Decor. TEPEE Cruet)

235
OPAL HERRINGBONE
(IGLOO Mold Cruet)

236
STARS & STRIPES
(Indiana Mold)

237
BLOWN OPAL DRAPERY
(Indiana Mold)

238
DAISY & FERN
(N. SWIRL Mold)

239
DAISY & FERN
(Spooner)

240
DAISY & FERN
(Creamer)

2½" W.

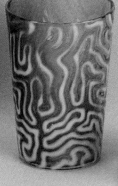

3¼" W.

241
OPALESCENT LATTICE
(Ribbed Pillar Mold)
(Sugar lid)

242
OPALESCENT HONEYCOMB
(Rainbow Tumbler)

243
RIBBED OPAL RINGS
(Tumbler)

244
SWIRLING MAZE
(Tumbler)

245
RIBBED OPAL LATTICE
(Sugar lid)

Miscellaneous Opalescent

246
OPALESCENT SWIRL
(Straw Jar)

247
**CONSOLIDATED
CRISS-CROSS**
(Ivy Ball)

248
COINSPOT

249
RIBBED OPAL RINGS
(Tankard)

250
COINSPOT & SWIRL
(Syrup)

251
RIBBED OPAL LATTICE
(Syrup)

252
BIG WINDOWS
(Syrup)

253
HOBNAIL
(Syrup)

254
CRISS-CROSS
(Mustard)

255
CONSOLIDATED
(Syrup)

256
OPALESCENT LATTICE
(Buckeye Sugar)

257
ROSE ONYX
(Sugar)

258
ROSE ONYX
(Mustard)

259
OPAL FERN
(Celery)

260
OPAL FERN
(Butter)

Miscellaneous Opalescent

261
COINSPOT
(WINDOWS Mold)

262
RIBBED COINSPOT
(Celery)

263
OPAL WINDOWS
(Night Lamp)

264
OPAL SEAWEED
(Night Lamp)

265
SCOTTISH MOOR
(Tankard)

266
COINSPOT
(Ring-Neck Syrup)

267
COINSPOT
(Nine-Panel Syrup)

268
COINSPOT
(Indiana Mold)

269
FENTON COIN DOT
(Cruet)

270
OPALESCENT DIAMONDS
(Cruet)

271
WIDE STRIPE
(Cruet)

272
OPALESCENT SWIRL
(ROYAL OAK Creamer)

273
RIBBED COINSPOT
(Sugar lid)

274
OPALES. HONEYCOMB
(½-pint pitcher)

275
BIG WINDOWS
(Sugar Shaker)

276
CHRYS. SWIRL
(Tall Salt)

277
POLKA DOT
(Sugar Shaker)

278
COINSPOT
(Water Bottle)

Opalescent by L.G. Wright
(Original Wright Names Used)

279
280
DAISY & FERN

281
OPAL SWIRL

282
EYE DOT

283
DIAMOND QUILTED

284
285
CHRISTMAS SNOWFLAKE

286
HONEYCOMB

287
HONEYCOMB

288
COINSPOT (OR OPAL DOT)

289 **HONEYCOMB**
290

291
EYE DOT

292
EYE DOT

293
HONEYCOMB

Opalescent by L.G. Wright
(Original Wright Names Used)

294	295	296	297	298	299
EYE DOT	**EYE DOT**	**DIAMOND QUILTED**	**HONEYCOMB**	**HONEYCOMB**	**HONEYCOMB**

300
ARS & STRIPES

301
EYE DOT

302
OPAL RIB

303
HOBNAIL
(Old)

304
HOBNAIL
(Wright)

305
HOBNAIL
(Czech)

306
DAISY & FERN

(Wright) **307 STARS & STRIPES** 308 (Old)

309
SWIRL

310
SWIRL

311
OPAL DOT

312
WINDOWS
(Old)

313
HONEYCOMB
(Wright)

101

Fenton Opalescent

314
SPIRAL OPTIC

315
SPIRAL OPTIC

316
SPIRAL OPTIC

317
DIAMOND QUILTED

318
COIN DOT

319
SPIRAL OPTIC
(Barcelona Mold)

320
SPIRAL OPTIC

321

322
POLKA DOT

323
SPIRAL OPTIC

324

325

326
POLKA DOT

327

328
SWIRLED FEATHER

329
DEVILBISS
(Perfume)

Experimental Opalescent by Fenton

(1978-1985)

330   331   332   333   334   335

336   337   338   339   340

341   342   343   344   345

Opalescent Lamps

by L.G. Wright

346

347

348

350

349

104

Opalescent Lamps
by
L.G. Wright

351

352

353

354

355

105

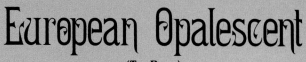

European Opalescent

(Top Rows)

&

Salt Shakers
(Bottom Row)

356
OPAL STRIPE
12″ English Vase)

357
OPAL OPTIC
(Gas Shade)

358
OPAL SWIRL
(Vase)

359
Iced Tea

360

361
(8½″ Vase)

362
(6″ pitcher)

363
(2½″ Tumbler)

364
(8″ Pitcher)

365
(5″ Tumbler)

366
(4½″ Rose Bowl)

367
NICKEL SWIRL
(Salt & Pepper)

368
WIDE STRIPE
(Salt Shaker)

369
POLKA DOT
(Salt & Pepper)

370
COINSPOT
(Salt & Pepper)

371
RIBBED COINSPOT
(Salt Shaker)

372
BUCKEYE LATTICE
(Salt & Pepper)

Miscellaneous Opalescent

373
DAISY & FERN
(14" Lustre)

374
SPIRAL OPTIC
(Fenton – 1939)

375

376
HOBNAIL
(Butter)

377
HOBNAIL
(5½" Milk Pitcher)

378
SWIRL
(Night Lamp)

379
WINDOWS
(7" Oil Lamp)

380
BUCKEYE LATTICE
(Creamer)

381
(Spooner)

382
SWIRL
(Cruet)

383
STRIPE
(Creamer)

384
DAISY & FERN
(Indiana Mold)

385
NAILSEA
(Fairy Lamp)

386
NAILSEA
(Fairy Lamp)

387
STRIPE
(9½" Bowl)

388
FERN
(Spooner)

389
FERN
(Salt)

390
FERN
(Sugar Lid)

391
LATTICE
(11" Bowl)

REPRODUCTIONS AND REINTRODUCTIONS

The difference between a reproduction and a "reintroduction" (a new terminology I am coining) is simple. A reproduction is a copy of an exact shape and color made much earlier by a non-existant factory. A reintroduction is simply taking an old design idea and placing it back on the giftware market in new shapes or in new colors never before made.

This section includes assorted reprints from the catalogues of the Fenton Art Glass Co., Williamstown, W. Va., and the L.G. Wright Glass Co., New Martinsville, W. Va. Fenton made almost all the cranberry opalescent offerred by L.G. Wright, a glass jobber firm which manufactured no actual glass (they did maintain a decorating force, however). Fenton built much of their business manufacturing "reintroductions" of old design ideas, but the firm did produce some "reproductions" as well. But since we are concerned here with cranberry opalescent, I will not delve into specifics. Most Fenton made since 1974 is trademarked. Anyone who collects Victorian blown opalescent, and who wishes to avoid buying Fenton reintroductions, must own copies of my two books covering Fenton's first fifty years.

The L.G. Wright Glass Co. built their business on reproductions. To be certain, they also produced "reintroductions" as well. Many old Victorian patterns were produced in colors and shapes never before made. If an item was never made in color by the original manufacturer, then that item is technically not a reproduction. Only the pattern is subject to reproduction—not the colored glass piece itself.

The Wright firm began business slowly during the 1930's and expanded during World War 2, after the purchase of many original molds from the Northwood-Dugan-Diamond factory at Indiana, Pa. During the war, the glass market in America faced no challenges from cheap European competitors, and Mr. Wright had much of his glass made by Fenton, which he in turn sold directly to his customers as

Two pages from a 1983 L.G. Wright catalogue showing many items in cranberry opalescent (Courtesy Steve Jennings)

his own glass. As the business grew, new molds were made, many of them reproducing the popular patterns of the period, WESTWARD HO, THREE FACE, MOON AND STAR and many others. The reproductions are almost identical to the originals, causing considerable confusion for beginner collectors.

Most of the cranberry opalescent being offerred by Wright was made from the old spot molds used by Northwood and Dugan at Indiana, Pa. OPAL STARS AND STRIPES seems to be the single exception. Some of the shape molds found there were also used. But in most cases, the Wright pieces were blown into their own shape molds, making these pieces easy to determine as "reintroductions". But there are a good number of exact reproductions, and differentiating these items from the originals is a matter of EXPERIENCE. Only an expert can tell you the difference, but you too can become an expert in time. There are almost no Wright reproductions which cannot be distinguished from old. The most difficult are the melon-rib barber bottle

(a few rare old examples do exist) and a few of their earliest water pitchers (from the 1940's) which now have more than forty years of age wear on the base.

Very little, if any, cranberry opalescent is being made by the Wright firm today, and their glass made from 1938 to 1980 has become very collectible in its own right. This glass is very expensive to make and in some cases a new piece retailed for almost as much as an astute collector could purchase an old example. But all cranberry, be it Victorian or reproduction or reintroduction, has value. It is up to the individual collector to determine the purity of his or her collection. I personally think age is only one key factor to a collection's value. Quality is another, and Fenton's quality is unquestionable.

On the other hand, there was some cranberry opalescent glass of limited quality made for A.A. Importing Co., which is heavy and poorly made. Only inexperienced or over-exuberant collectors have been stung by these cheap reproductions.

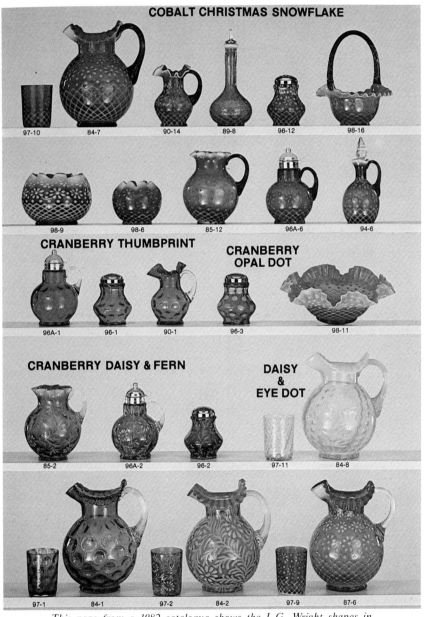

This page from a 1982 catalogue shows the L.G. Wright shapes in CHRISTMAS SNOWFLAKE and the newly released DAISY AND EYE DOT (the latter called FLORAL EYELET on page 49 in finish cruet, all by Hobbs Glass Co. The celery vase is similar in shape to the one known in SCOTTISH MOOR, but Percy Beaumont worked for Hobbs and could have copied the shape for West Virginia's line

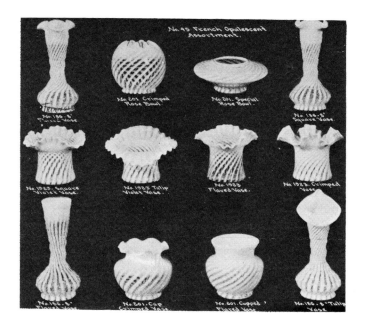

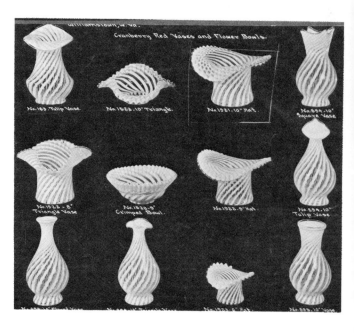

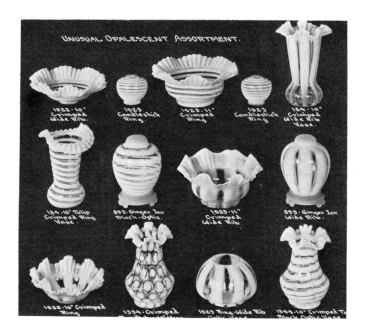

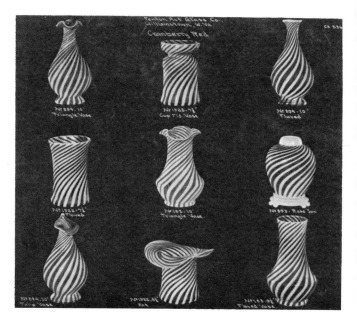

The above are reprints from four catalogue sales sheets showing some of Fenton's blown opalescent from the 1930's. The "Unusual Opalescent Assortment", which is known mostly in white, is dated Circa 1939 in F2. However, there is conflicting evidence that this may date as early as 1933, when a water set in FENTON'S RING appeared in trade journal announcements. A number of lines in white opalescent pressed ware were also released in "french opalescent" at about this time. Fenton's blown No. 1934 Liquor bottle is known with opalescent stripes, and this was made in 1934. Apparently Fenton did not make any cranberry opalescent until 1938 or 1939, about the time L.G. Wright had his HOBNAIL barber bottle reproduced by them.

Blown Opalescent

SHARDS FROM INDIANA, PA.
(Northwood/National/Dugan)

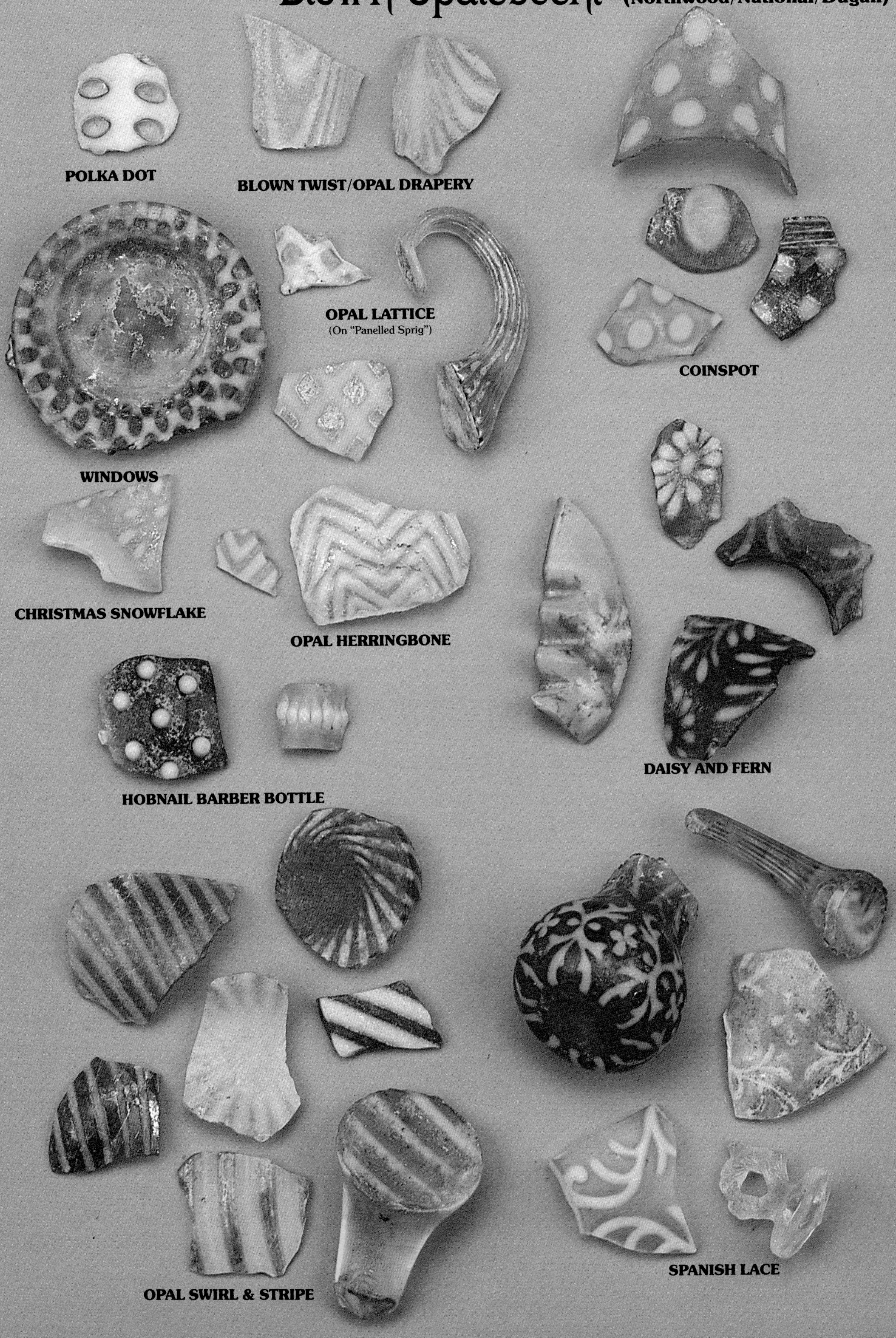

POLKA DOT

BLOWN TWIST/OPAL DRAPERY

COINSPOT

WINDOWS

OPAL LATTICE
(On "Panelled Sprig")

CHRISTMAS SNOWFLAKE

OPAL HERRINGBONE

DAISY AND FERN

HOBNAIL BARBER BOTTLE

SPANISH LACE

OPAL SWIRL & STRIPE